Stupefaction

Stupefaction

A Radical Anatomy of Phantoms

KESTON SUTHERLAND

LONDON NEW YORK CALCUTTA

Seagull Books 2011

© Keston Sutherland 2011

ISBN   978 1 9064 9 797 2

British Library Cataloguing-in-Publication Data
A catalogue record for this book is available
from the British Library

Typeset by Seagull Books, Calcutta, India
Printed and bound by Hyam Enterprises, Calcutta, India

For Jenny Greenshields and J. H. Prynne

Contents

Acknowledgements

I'm grateful to all the following friends, colleagues and editors for conversation, critical response, enthusiasm and encouragement that helped toward making this book: Ruth Abbott, Tariq Ali, Jennifer Bajorek, Nathan Takamura, Peter Boxall, Andrea Brady, Stuart Calton, Sara Crangle, Matt ffytche, Gordon Finlayson, William Fuller, Jenny Greenshields, Danny Hayward, Moira Herbst, Simon Jarvis, Daniel Kane, Naveen Kishore, Josh Kotin, Sam Ladkin, Vicky Lebeau, Philip Newman, Peter Nicholls, Ian Patterson, Neil Pattison, Brian Price, J. H. Prynne, Robin Purves, John David Rhodes, Nicholas Royle, Eirik Steinhoff, George Sutherland, Meghan Sutherland, Suzanne Sutherland, Zoe Sutherland, Jow Walton and John Wilkinson. My thanks also to the poets, some of them mentioned already in the list above, who have filled the UK, and especially Brighton, Cambridge and London, as well as Cork in Ireland, with readings, books, journals, arguments, criticism and comradeship, and who have together created what remain the primary social scenes of my critical thinking. There are, happily, far too many to mention them all, but I would like especially to thank Sean Bonney, Rosy Carrick, Jennifer Cooke, Martin Corless-Smith, Jimmy Cummins, Ryan Dobran, Chris Goode, Jeremy Hardingham, Alan Hay, Trevor Joyce, Justin Katko, Jonny Liron, Francesca Lisette, Joseph Luna, Peter Manson, Marianne Morris, Richard Parker, Luke Roberts, Josh Stanley, Jonty Tiplady, Mike Wallace-Hadrill and Rachel Warriner. Finally, my thanks to all my students at the University of Sussex for six years of discussion, discovery and happiness.

Introduction

> For a wise man, it is not enough to study nature and
> the truth; he must dare to proclaim it for the benefit
> of the small number of those who are willing and able
> to think; for the others, who are the willing slaves of
> prejudice, are no more capable of reaching the truth
> than are frogs of flying.
>
> Julien Offray de la Mettrie
> *Machine Man*

In *The Rules of Art*, the great French sociologist of culture
Pierre Bourdieu described the sort of book he loved. 'I
delight in those books in which theory, because it is the air
one breathes, is everywhere and nowhere—in the detour
of a note, in the commentary on an old text or in the very
structure of interpretative discourse.'[1] *Stupefaction: A Radical Anatomy of Phantoms* is about how theory may be
found nowhere. It is a study of poetic and philosophical
practices that can be relied on to disclose the absolute destitution of truth in objects, uses of language, persons and
lives. What use might it be to a poet or philosopher to
represent things 'in the most contemptible and insignificant point of view', as William Hazlitt considered that

Alexander Pope typically did, or to assert that the majority of people may no more be worked upon 'with fine Sense' than a brick may be hewn 'with a razor', as Pope supposed?[2] What does it mean to decide that a proposition is absolutely false, or that a poem is absolutely worthless or absolutely not beautiful, or that a person is compulsorily incapable of seeing things for what they are, or of acting in any other way besides in blind, reflex promotion of his own interests? What possibilities for thinking, relating and expressing are realized or defined by the belief that we share our world with 'slaves of prejudice [...] no more capable of reaching the truth than are frogs of flying'?

That phrase of De la Mettrie's is a fairly aggressive example of the sort of observation I am interested in, but not an extreme example. Neither is aggression of his sort anachronistic from the perspective of contemporary poetic and philosophical thinking. Right up to our present moment, philosophy and poetry continue to identify the objects, relations, persons and lives that can be thought about and described, as well as the audiences that can be expected to understand what philosophy and poetry are, and what they are doing, by defining the identity of the person who is excluded from truth, or the language that is destitute of truth, or the life that cannot be lived rightly. It is an important distinction for this book that a person may on the one hand be doubted to possess the sort of mind that is necessary for truth, and on the other be categorically ruled out from possession of truth. Similarly, a poem may on the one hand be doubted to have anything beautiful in it, or on the other the absolute value of truth in a poem may be fixed at nil. I am interested in the doubtfulness of beauty but do not discuss it directly until the last chapter of this book; the first three chapters are a series of attempts to think about the emphatic ruling out of beauty, the definition of experiences of thinking and reactions to art that are unalterably inert and must never be allowed to lead anywhere, and the significance (in particular the social and political significance for people living under capitalism) of identifying the type of enemy existence by defining it as irremediably destitute of truth.

The central and heroic figure in the book is Karl Marx. It will be clear from my readings of Marx that I am not arguing that the philosopher or poet is simply biting the air, or fighting with a straw man, or fabricating a stupefied identity out of the 'fine Web of his Soul' in order that he may angrily tear it down for being nothing but a web.[3] On the contrary, my suggestion is that some of the most brilliantly illuminating criticism of social reality has depended on the nomination of an identity for absolute stupefaction, and that this nomination has more often been powerfully illuminating when it has been conscious

3

and emphatic rather than unconscious or surreptitious. Marx certainly knew that he was nominating thousands of real people for the role of the compulsorily and irremediably stupefied individual; Adorno knew that he was nominating billions. How many other lives in dim expression were consigned to universal darkness along with Richard Blackmore's, when Pope wrote his *Peri Bathous: Art of Sinking in Poetry* (1727)? When Wordsworth in his 'Preface' to *Lyrical Ballads* tried to distinguish himself absolutely from 'Poets, and Men ambitious of the fame of Poets' who, by setting themselves to 'mechanical adoption' of the language of poetry without 'being animated by the same passion' as genuine poets, had produced a language 'differing materially from the real language of men in *any situation*',[4] this was in part a way of defining a social identity which must have no place on this world, which is the world of all of us, in which to find its happiness through the expression of gratitude for beauty. It was also a way of suggesting how a language belonging to men might be other than 'real'. These authors are the focus of my study, because, for one thing, I think each of them is incomprehensible without some effort to reflect on the meaning of stupefaction for their work; they also were among the greatest and most original anatomists of the identity of the stupefied individual. I write about Marx, Pope and Wordsworth also for the reason that I love them for everything I have learned from them, and for inspiring me to believe that I will learn from them forever.

But many other writers and thinkers could have been chosen. The theme is an enormous one. This book is not even the lineaments of a comprehensive theoretical account of stupefaction; it is a sequence of essays that try in different ways to think about the consequences for poetry and philosophy of a specific act of identification. If it were a survey or general history instead, its task would be as perfectly inexhaustible as the researches of Bouvard and Pécuchet. A survey could hardly avoid a long account of Nietzsche's philosophy, which is so intensely dependent on its pageant of idiots that it couldn't exist for a single untimely moment without them. It would find that the same is true for Pound's poetry and essays, which everywhere project, mock and vilify the halfwit incapable of being bucked up by beauty, hearing the subtle measure of Pound's verse, or correctly despising Carlo Dolci, as the perennial 'Mr. Buggins' cannot.[5] Gillian Rose's account of 'Holocaust piety' depends on fashioning an identity called 'the ultimate predator', who might very well be us (who else?).[6] Heidegger nominated lizards, who must not be allowed unrestricted access even to the sun since they are not ontological. He also diverted the reptilian advances of 'natural science', and of psychoanalysis in particular (psychoanalysis being the bathos of natural science), onto an old beaten track safely wide of *Dasein*. When Heidegger hears 'most people grant that the central characteristic of being human cannot be approached by natural science', most people are, in his estimation, absolutely right for once, albeit at the inconvenience for most people of becoming ventriloquist's dummies whose 'central characteristic of being human' has been selected for them by Heidegger.[7] Hegel livens up the great 'Preface' to his *Phenomenology of Spirit* by ushering on stage the 'dullard' with his 'untutored mind' ('Wie stumpf müßte der Kopf seyn'). The untutored dullard or thickhead is not a person excluded from formal education but a philosopher who crampingly restricts thinking to 'formalism' and the 'construction' of propositions taken for truths. His mental fuss over 'a synoptic table like a skeleton with scraps of paper stuck all over it, or like rows of closed and labelled boxes in a grocer's stall' is the picture of spirit condemned to a rest-stop on the way of despair, idly browsing the stalls.[8] Whitman, who is an especially beautiful case, identifies *no one on earth*—or, at least, no one on American earth—as the limited and incapable person that poetry must depend on for its cosmic availability. Lacan as if straightforwardly ejects 'idiots' from the seminar: 'Do not, however, get the idea that I address myself to everyone at large. I am speaking to those who are savvy, to the non-idiots,' writes the psychotherapist in the spirit of clinical benevolence, echoing De la Mettrie.[9] Douglas Oliver, one of the most interesting poets who wrote in English in the last century, was determined to make the stupid individual merge as far as possible into himself. 'The task I set myself,' he wrote in a letter to his friend and fellow poet Peter Riley, in reference to his recently completed *The Harmless Building* (1972), 'was to write a stupid book.' If he could do that, he might be spared the identity of the 'left-wing poets' who are 'intellectual snobs', whose 'structures' are 'carefully cemented so that no one should see through their gaps'. Poets whose artifice is motivated by the anxiety to keep gaps from being seen through are in Oliver's view generally 'concerned to tell other people *exactly* how it is'; they are also 'the heroes of their own poems all the time'.[10] What these widely different thinkers all share is a commitment to literalizing the figure of the stupefied individual into a real person (him, you, them, me, us); this book is a study of that specific act of literalization and its significance for art and for a critique of social relations.

My subtitle, 'a radical anatomy of phantoms', may be explained in part by a brief attempt to distinguish my reading of Marx from the influential reading by Derrida in *Specters of Marx*. For Derrida, one of the most important problems with phantoms is that there is a type of philosopher who will not believe in them. 'A traditional scholar', or rather, since Derrida's use of an English word in italics cannot be unimportant for his identification of this stupefied figure, the '*scholar* traditionnel', as the figure is named in French, 'does not believe in ghosts—nor in all that could be called the virtual space of spectrality'.[11] Marx, it turns out, is something like this '*scholar* traditionnel'; he is obsessed with phantoms and with the spectral objectivity of commodities, but will not believe in them.

> Marx does not like ghosts any more than do his adversaries. He does not want to believe in them. But he thinks of nothing else. He believes rather in what is supposed to distinguish them from actual reality, living effectivity. He believes he can oppose them, like life to death, like vain appearances of the simulacrum to real presence. He believes enough in the dividing line of this opposition to want to denounce, chase away or exorcise the spectres but by means of critical analysis and not by some counter-magic. But how to distinguish between the analysis that denounces magic and the counter-magic that it still risks being?[12]

The Marx who emerges in this picture (which sounds curiously like a trailer for a film whose central character is 'Marx': the philosophy of the 'to come' as enticement without spoilers) is an obsessive compulsive, activated by a deeply instinctive 'hostility toward ghosts, a terrified hostility that sometimes fends off terror with a burst of laughter' and that keeps him from acknowledging how unworkable is his distinction between death and life, or between dead and living labour (it is unworkable by being dependent on an ontology of presence). This blindness in hostility is what Marx 'will always have had in common with his adversaries'. Derrida's response to this traditional and scholarly obsession is to make Marx into the object of psychoanalysis. His 'attempted radicalization of Marxism' is conducted by literalizing Marx into the person of the analysand.[13] For Derrida, Marx was not the rational satirist of phantomatic speculative thinking he took himself to be; rather, he was condemned by a predeconstructive ontology to repress what was most obvious to him, namely, that phantoms are not opposite to reality. His 'burst of laughter' is not identified by Derrida as satire, nor is it the 'sovereign' burst of laughter which, according to an earlier essay by Derrida, 'alone exceeds dialectics and the dialectician'. Instead, Marx's laughter is a psychic defence.[14] Marx 'loved the figure of the ghost, he detested it, he called it to witness his contestation, he was haunted by it, harassed, besieged, obsessed by it'. He went 'to desperate lengths [. . .] to try to distinguish between spirit and specter'. Above all, Marx remained predeconstructive by failing to see that 'the difference between specter and spirit [. . .] is a differ*a*nce,' and by therefore being unable to accept the ineradicability of ghosts and unable to think in 'fear'; he cannot think in fear because 'fear is not good for the serenity of research and the analytic distinction of concepts.'[15] Marx, apparently, was protecting his serenity by repressing his fear of ghosts. That Freudian order of psychic priority (serenity first, reality later) makes Marx into just another 'Hero of Truth' (to borrow a phrase from Wordsworth's early poem 'Adventures on Salisbury Plain'): despite his complex and tormenting passion for the very figure which he cannot help but repressively mock, the *fantôme* or *spectre*, Marx allowed his critique of speculative philosophy to boil down to yet another dismissal of superstition in the old Republican or Enlightenment style of Paine or Condorcet. Marx missed the chance really to think spectrality (which would have allowed him to overcome the deterministic tendencies in his thinking about the future) because he was too *protective* of his, in truth, merely 'analytic' distinction between the living and the dead. In reply to this obsessively self-protective Marx, Derrida calls for 'a deconstruction of the critical limits, the reassuring limits that guarantee the necessary and legitimate exercise of critical questioning'.[16]

My own reading of Marx is very different from this one by Derrida. I think that Marx had an understanding of 'critical limits' considerably more complex than Derrida will accept from his analysand; Derrida the clinician is perhaps not sufficiently stimulated to counter-transference. For Marx, critical limits were not simply stops in the flow of thought, boundaries imposed on criticism by an ontology of presence, comforts against anxiety, or points at which to find rational thinking exhausted. Critical limits are for Marx a kind of cognitive testimony of social facts, the measuring up of thinking to injustice; they are ineliminable from the conceptual account of the necessity of communism. Without what Derrida diagnostically identified as the 'reassuring limits that guarantee the necessary and legitimate exercise of critical questioning', there could be no ruthless criticism of everything in existence. Marx's 'ruthless criticism of everything in existence' is made ruthless by the conscious adoption of limits (in the form of social contradictions) that define the *social* act of transgression from criticism into ideology.[17] This must seem an unsophisticated account of criticism if what we are interested in instead is a style of thinking that allows us to deny the status of 'legitimacy' to any act of conceptual or interpretive limitation by deciding, for example, that critical limits and legitimate thinking were always already the same thing, so that there can be only a tautological relation between them. But that style of thinking, though preferable for its more nearly infinite patience with intricacy, may in turn be literalized into the person (an analysand, if we like) who from anxiety and hostility is made blind to his own 'fear' of a concept that was absolutely central to everything Marx ever wrote, namely, the concept of class. Derrida is not interested in class, in *Specters of Marx*, but only in the already universal condition of the subject that 'phantomalizes' itself. There is no such thing as bourgeois consciousness and no limit is proved to be inescapable by its truth to living social contradiction, so that 'limits' in general may be those altogether more pliable and curable things, psychic deceptions contrived for the purpose of reassuring ourselves (for example, that death is absolutely different from life, or that philosophy is absolutely different from ideology). We may then believe that if we could only give up defending ourselves against our own living phantomaticity with the pikes and pepper sprays of mockery, the scholasticism of these distinctions could be exploded by a properly sovereign burst of laughter that 'exceeds dialectics'.[18] Another way of putting that is to say that for Derrida in *Specters of Marx*, limits are that ambivalently both figural and objective thing which deconstructive philosophy must invoke in order to offer a more sublime reassurance than the scholastic analysand could ever wish to profit by, the reassurance that all limits have already been transgressed or already 'will have' been.

Marx is, by comparison, a fiercely unreassuring thinker. For Marx, philosophy begins when we recognize 'reassuring limits that guarantee the necessary and legitimate exercise of critical questioning' for what they are: not fictions adopted by philosophers to protect the serenity necessary for research and its clarity of analytic distinctions but relations in the world to be demolished. From the perspective of a 'ruthless criticism of everything in existence', Derrida's *limites rassurantes* are not cognitive figures or analytic devices that philosophy may invoke in order to deny, transgress or multiply them on the authority of its own ingenuity, but social facts that must be confrontationally insisted upon. They reassure you of the fact that you are eating your brothers and sisters and that no act of deconstruction (or any other sort of protest against being too narrowly identified, however brilliant) will get humanity out of your mouth. That paradigmatic form of consumption is the subject of the first chapter of this book. Derrida calls his anti-Leninist critique of Marx 'de-limitation', 'the infinite opening of all these borders'.[19] For Marx, there is no such thing as *ouverture infinie* and it is not the purpose of radical philosophy to 'de-limit' anything. *Ouverture infinie* is the bourgeois concept par excellence; its terminal apotheosis is the global free market.

Das Kapital is a 'book in which theory, because it is the air one breathes, is everywhere and nowhere'. It is also more than that. It is a book that cannot be identified by an encomium. But if an encomium may nonetheless make a start toward identifying *Das Kapital*, then this description by Bourdieu, a description of who knows how many unnamed books delighted in by one individual, seems as good a place to start as any. The Marx I admire in this book was not simply a theorist but a great writer, in particular a great writer of satire; possibly he was, in a special sense, the greatest satirist of his and our time. Like 'the air one breathes', satire in Marx is everywhere and nowhere. It is nowhere, if Marx can be made a purely theoretical author, or *Das Kapital* in essence a purely theoretical text; it is everywhere, if the type of objectivity argued for in *Das Kapital* is incompatible with bourgeois theoretical variations on the 'concepts' in that book, and if even 'Marxist' readers are not invited by the book into a relationship of sympathetic mutuality with its author but are themselves the compulsorily cannibalistic objects of its most disgusting and confounding social analysis. Satire is nowhere, if Marx's often unbearably overextended and repetitious attacks on bad speculative thinking, or 'German philosophy', in his early writing can be trimmed down to nothing but the messy commencement of 'historical materialism', or the achievement of standing Hegel on his head; it is everywhere, if the most bullying denunciations of the concept and practice of speculative thinking in Marx's early writing are, in fact, the revival of that concept and practice, not simply because the denunciations help clear the way for dialectic to be made useful for historical materialism but because the effort (overflowing over

14

hundreds of pages) to make 'the semblance of a fight' into a real fight by the stretching out of mockery beyond excess was truly the most 'strenuous effort of the concept' that Marx could then make.

By misidentifying Marx's satire as laughter designed to 'fend off' phantoms, Derrida obscures a distinction that is crucial to my own account of Marx. The distinction I mean is between Marx's criticism of 'speculative constructions' and his criticism of 'metaphysics'. These are not the same thing for Marx, not least because *they cannot be the same object of satire*. Marx satirized 'speculative constructions' in the writing of the so-called Critical Critics or Young Hegelians not simply for inaccuracy in social diagnosis, but for lacking any sort of confrontational truth. I describe this satire in Chapter 3, in connection with Pope's invention of the concept of 'bathos'. But by repetitiously and unrelentingly satirizing 'speculative constructions' Marx learned a new use for them. By anatomizing the dead art of inferior poets, Pope refined the living art of making ugly and ridiculous lines of verse; by his cruelly untiring, comically repetitive demolition of the speculative constructions of inferior Hegelian philosophers, Marx refined the art of making satirical speculative constructions. The fruit was *Das Kapital*. The 'bourgeoisie' in *Das Kapital* is not only a real, living class but also a satirical 'speculative construction'; its existence as a 'speculative construction' is incomprehensible except by the illumination of confrontational truth by satire. Speculative constructions, then—and I drop the quotation marks here demonstratively—are not excluded from social reality (even if social reality may be reduced to 'presence'), for example, by 'reassuring limits' in thinking, but they are a major, living part of social reality. Real individuals live out their lives as speculative constructions. This is not a joke for Marx, simply, or just a paradox designed to make thinking more contradictory: it is a 'social fact'. This book makes some suggestions about what it may mean to decide that something is a 'fact'. What it meant for Marx in this case was the definition of a social necessity, the destruction of capitalist relations of production and capitalist social relations. The definition of that necessity entailed the emphatic and unapologetic identification of speculative constructions with reality, in particular with the real lives of living individuals. The capitalist *is* a personification, despite our contriving to believe that he is a person, too; the satire in that identification is not reducible to an 'irony' that can be deleted without loss of truth from Marx's empiricism but is the literary basis of Marx's dialectical materialist objectivity. There are human beings who are phantoms as well as flesh, for Marx as well as for Derrida; but, unlike Derrida, Marx did not consider that their existence amounted to a reason to believe in them.

Metaphysics is, by comparison, not indeed a trivial object of satire for Marx but one he uses more narrowly. Commodities are 'metaphysical', but this is a consequence of the existence in society of human relations that are speculatively constructed; humans are not themselves metaphysical for Marx, except in their commodity form as wage labour. Marx's critique of political economy is one that, in Derrida's words, 'purports to be a surpassing of Hegelianism'. But whereas for Derrida that purpose must imply (or may even be defined as) the ambition to arrive at 'a science free of metaphysics [affranchie de la métaphysique]', Marx did not think that getting past Hegel must mean getting rid of metaphysics.[20] He did not, for two reasons. First, because 'metaphysics' still had important work to do: it had to be satirized into a new actuality. Marx *reinstated* metaphysics as an object of satire in his analysis of the 'secret' of the fetish character of commodities in *Das Kapital*. I suggest in Chapter 1 that this was not the attempt to purge philosophy of a revenant, for example by invoking metaphysics in order then to abolish it; rather, it was a new literary invention, a culinary metaphysics for savvy consumers whose taste in injustice was sufficiently refined to make naked inhumanity too bland. Second, getting past Hegel did not mean getting past metaphysics any more than getting past Epicurus meant getting past Epicurus' account of the behaviour of atoms, because the purpose of getting past Hegel was to define the necessity of communism and to insist that philosophical truth must be confrontational. Enfranchisement by rejection of metaphysics is no sort of enfranchisement at all, for Marx.

Marx's speculative constructions are profoundly at odds with the society they nonetheless intensely adequate and anatomize. A 'radical anatomy' in my sense, which I believe I owe to Marx, is one that is profoundly at odds with the real identity it defines and uncovers in detail. The body I lay bare is not the naked object my disclosing allows me to look at. Its irrecusable disarticulation from social reality is the truth of materialist dialectic.

This book is about beauty as well as social truth. I hope it is a book in which theory may be found everywhere and nowhere. Its last chapter is an effort to think about how that could happen, how we can make it happen, not in thought alone but on the world and as our happiness.

Notes

1. Pierre Bourdieu, *The Rules of Art: Genesis and Structure of the Literary Field* (Susan Emanuel trans.) (Cambridge: Polity, 2005), p. 178.

2. The quotations are from William Hazlitt on Alexander Pope, and from Pope himself. 'On the Question whether Pope was a Poet' (1818) in Duncan Wu (ed.), *The Selected Writings of William Hazlitt*, VOL. 9 (London: Pickering and Chatto, 1998), p. 27; 'Thoughts on Various Subjects' in *The Prose Works of Alexander Pope, Volume 2: The Major Works, 1725–1744* (Rosemary Cowler ed.) (Oxford: Blackwell, 1986), p. 151.

3. The phrase is from a letter by John Keats. Here it is in its original context:

   > Now it appears to me that almost any Man may like the spider spin from his own inwards his own airy Citadel—the points of leaves and twigs on which the spider begins her work are few, and she fills the air with a beautiful circuiting. Man should be content with as few points to tip with the fine Web of his Soul, and weave a tapestry empyrean full of symbols for his spiritual eye, of softness for his spiritual touch, of space for his wandering, of distinctness for his luxury [*The Letters of John Keats* (Maurice Buxton Forman ed.), 3rd edn (London: Oxford University Press, 1947), p. 103].

4. William Wordsworth, *The Prose Works of William Wordsworth* (W. J. B. Owen and Jane Worthington Smyser eds), VOL. 1 (Oxford: Oxford University Press, 1974), p. 186.

5. 'Hang a painting by Carlo Dolci beside a Cosimo Tura. You cannot prevent Mr. Buggins from preferring the former.' [Ezra Pound, *ABC of Reading* (London: Faber & Faber, 1991 [1934]), p. 26.]

6. Gillian Rose, *Mourning Becomes the Law: Philosophy and Representation* (Cambridge: Cambridge University Press, 1996), p. 47ff.

7. Martin Heidegger, *Zollikon Seminars* (Medard Boss ed., Franz Mayr and Richard Askay trans.) (Evanston: Northwestern University Press, 2001), p. 27. Maurice Merleau-Ponty similarly condemns natural science to a mere insightless 'manipulation' of objects in the first sentence of his excellent essay, 'Eye and Mind', in *Maurice Merleau-Ponty: Basic Writings* (Thomas Baldwin ed.) (London: Routledge, 2003), p. 291. The exaltation of phenomenology to the status of provider of primordial disclosure and unconcealment has from Husserl onwards consistently depended on the construction of pejorative accounts of natural science and psychoanalysis.

8. G. W. F. Hegel, *Phenomenology of Spirit* (A. V. Miller trans.) (Oxford: Oxford University Press, 1977), pp. 30–1, 37–8; *Gesammelte Werke* (Wolfgang Bonsiepen and Reinhard Heede eds), VOL. 9 (Hamburg: Felix Meiner Verlag, 1980), p. 51. Cf. 'Differenz des Fichte'schen und Schelling'schen Systems der Philosophie' (Differences in Fichte's and Schelling's Systems of Philosophy) in *Gesammelte Werke* (Hartmut Buchner and Otto Pöggeler eds) *Band 4: Jenaer Kritische Schriften* (Hamburg: Felix Meiner Verlag, 1968), p. 9, where Hegel says that 'Spirit'

slips through the fingers of the inquirer preoccupied with the mummies and heaps of contingencies that are the dead objects of philosophy reduced to mere information gathering. For a tendentious confirmation of this identity for stupefaction in philosophy, cf. Martin Heidegger, *Hegel's 'Phenomenology of Spirit'* (Parvis Emad and Kenneth Maly trans.) (Bloomington: Indiana University Press, 1994), p. 31.

9. Jacques Lacan, *Television: A Challenge to the Psychoanalytic Establishment* (Joan Copjec ed., Denis Hollier, Rosalind Kraus and Annette Michelson trans.) (New York: Norton, 1990), p. 3.

10. Douglas Oliver, letter to Peter Riley, 31 December 1970. Quoted by permission of Peter Riley.

11. Jacques Derrida, *Specters of Marx: The State of the Debt, the Work of Mourning, and the New International* (Peggy Kamuf trans.) (New York: Routledge, 2006), p. 12. Cf. Jacques Derrida, *Of Spirit: Heidegger and the Question* (Geoffrey Bennington and Rachel Bowlby trans.) (Chicago: University of Chicago Press, 1991), p. 42, where Derrida identifies (I think more persuasively) the 'teacher of philosophy' as the type of 'traditional scholar' who thinks that the role of the philosopher must be as 'the functionary of the fundamental'. For an elucidating affirmation of Derrida's view in *Specters of Marx* that 'life must be open to death,' and that Marx's writing may be criticized for forcing a closure between the two, cf. Martin Hägglund, *Radical Atheism: Derrida and the Time of Life* (Stanford: Stanford University Press, 2008), p. 43.

This criticism of Marx seems wayward to me, not simply because the distinction between life and death in *Das Kapital* is unintelligible except in the context of an analysis of class relations which Derrida emphatically omits ('dead labour' and 'living labour' are descriptions belonging to a specific anatomy of social relations) but also because both Derrida and Hägglund suggest that because he depends on a rigid distinction between life and death, Marx may be contradicted by the 'assertion', as Hägglund names it, that 'life must be open to death.' But that assertion does not, in my view, contradict or even significantly bear on Marx's account of the rigid distinction between life and death. Literalized into Marx's terms, the injunction to keep life open to death would mean for the factory worker that she must keep her labour time open to the commodity that is the alienated product of that time, and that she must likewise keep her human potential as she may experience it beyond the coercions of wage labour open to her mechanical activity at work. Whatever might be the meaning of that 'openness' for a criticism of the ontology of presence, it is difficult to see what its meaning could be for the worker, who may think that she can hardly avoid being 'open' to the most invasive objects and coercions in her life. I also dispute Hägglund's view that his logical retelling of *Specters of Marx* (and of all Derrida's work) can rule out, strictly on logical grounds, any and all religious meaning for Derrida's use of the word 'messianism'. Hägglund offers to explain why Derrida uses the word but only suggests that a 'radical atheism' like Derrida's 'cannot simply denounce messianic hope as an illusion' but must 'show that messianic hope does not stem from a hope for immortality (the positive infinity of eternity) but from a hope for survival (the negative infinity of time)' (ibid., p. 136). But Hägglund's own 'crucial question', as he calls it, remains unanswered: Why retain the word 'messianic'? Why not instead allow philosophy to be identical to its logical restatement, by talking only about 'hope that does not stem from a hope for immortality' rather than about 'messianic hope'? Is Derrida fending off immortality with a burst of religiosity?

12. Derrida, *Specters of Marx*, pp. 57–8.

13. Ibid., pp. 58, 115.

14. Neither is Marx's 'burst of laughter' allowed to be anything as complex as the sovereign burst of laughter which 'alone exceeds dialectics and the dialectician' (by way of being uncontainable within Hegel's panlogicistic philosophy) in Derrida's 'From Restricted to General Economy: A Hegelianism Without Reserve'. Cf. Jacques Derrida, *Writing and Difference* (Alan Bass trans.) (London: Routledge, 2002), p. 323ff. Because Marx's laughter is still dialectical, it cannot be so explosive as that of Bataille.

15. Derrida, *Specters of Marx*, pp. 132, 153, 170, 218.

16. Ibid., p. 204.

17. The clearest statement of this necessity as a necessity for thinking is by Lukács:

> The bourgeoisie possesses only the semblance of a human existence. A living contradiction must necessarily arise between semblance and reality, for

every individual of the bourgeois class, and it is to a great extent dependent on the individual himself whether he pacifies this contradiction using the means of ideological deception that his class constantly presses onto him, or whether this contradiction remains alive within him and leads to him tearing up the deceptive integuments of bourgeois ideology, either completely or at least in part' ['Marx and the Problem of Ideological Decay' (1938) in *Essays on Realism* (Rodney Livingstone ed., David Fernbach trans.) (London: Lawrence and Wishart, 1980), p. 133].

Lukács here takes a more pastoral interest in the welfare of the bourgeois individual than will often be found in Marx. The suggestion that contradiction must 'remain alive' within the individual means that it will otherwise be dead in him. Contradiction cannot simply be ruled out, discredited as the object or noumenon of a merely formal dialectics, or replaced by a more profitably subtilisable concept like difference; when contradiction is denied, it doesn't disappear but becomes necrotic (dead contradiction is the bathos of living humanity).

18. Derrida, *Writing and Difference*, p. 323.

19. Derrida, *Specters of Marx*, pp. 204, 209. The fundamental anti-Leninism of *Specters of Marx* unmistakably emerges from a comparison of Derrida's book with (for example) Lenin's essay 'The Three Sources and Three Component Parts of Marxism' (1913). Though he does not criticize Lenin directly, Derrida makes it the special

effort of his text to reject the firm Leninist view that (1) 'The Marxian doctrine [. . .] provides men with an integral world conception which is irreconcilable with any form of superstition, reaction, or defence of bourgeois oppression;' (2) 'Marx's philosophy is finished philosophical materialism' (for Derrida, we may not speak of a finished philosophy, except in self-reassurance); and (3) 'People always were and always will be the stupid victims of deceit and self-deceit in politics until they learn to discover the *interests* of some class behind all moral, religious, political and social phrases, declarations and promises.' That last conviction of Lenin's (and Marx's), if we wish to accept it, must hold for deconstruction too: from a Leninist perspective, the philosopher will remain a 'stupid victim of deceit' (he will be the identity for stupefaction) until he discovers to himself and to public view the class interests behind his thinking and behind the culture of friendship that sustains it. Cf. *The Essentials of Lenin in Two Volumes*, VOL. 1 (London: Lawrence and Wishart, 1947), pp. 59–63.

20. Jacques Derrida, 'The Pit and the Pyramid: Introduction to Hegel's Semiology' in *Margins of Philosophy* (Alan Bass trans.) (New York: Harvester Wheatsheaf, 1982), p. 75; *Marges de la philosophie* (Paris: Minuit, 1972), p. 86.

Marx in Jargon

FIRST TERM: 'BOURGEOISDOM'

> If ever Buffon's word was true of any man it was in
> regard to Marx: The style is the man—the style of
> Marx is Marx.
>
> Wilhelm Liebknecht
> *Karl Marx: Biographical Memoirs*[1]

In his 1873 preface to the second edition of *Das Kapital*,
Marx gives a brief report on the fortunes of his 'critique of
political economy' following its first submission to the
public in 1867. The report is compact and polemical, dis-
missing in style the substance of a few representatively
negative reviews, succinctly exposing their arguments for
mere squabblings and detractions 'with the skill of a great
master of verbal fence', as his English gentlemen con-
tenders may have thought.[2] The report describes not
workers' reactions to *Das Kapital* but reactions in the
bourgeois press, the official taste-making organs of 'Bürg-
erthum und seinen doktrinären Wortführrern', 'the bourgeoisie and its doctrinaire spokesmen'. This was Marx's

acidic motto for opponents from both the right and the left, both the celebrant practitioners of uncritical 'political economy' and their unwitting satirist sidekicks among the fashionable German peddlers of 'dialectic in its mystified form'. In the first English translation of 1886, Samuel Moore and Edward Aveling translate the motto as 'bourgeoisdom and its doctrinaire professors'. 'Bourgeoisdom' is not a word that could have tripped lightly from the lips of Marx's Victorian English readers. They had not read it before. Moore and Aveling's is the first recorded use in English. *Bourgeoisdom*. The word is cumbersome, dull, conspicuously jargonistic, not in any language, stupidly weighed down with the echo of the German *dumm* (stupid), not to mention English boredom. Why did Moore and Aveling invent it? Why sharpen the satiric ring of Marx's phrase? Not, presumably, in order to change the content of a proposition belonging to Marx but, on the contrary, so as to be sure to preserve it. Marx's English translators wanted English readers for Marx. To make sure that those readers would be reading Marx, and not some bad equivalent of Marx, the English translators in this instance rewrote Marx in jargon. (The twentieth-century translator of *Das Kapital* into English, Ben Fowkes, cleaned out the jargon by reverting to the better established 'bourgeoisie'.)[3] Moore and Aveling's version is in this instance jargonistic where the original is not. But the translators must presumably have felt that, far from taking any liberty with Marx's text or departing from the spirit of it, they had kept that spirit alive. There may be just a little more of Marx in 'bourgeoisdom' than in 'bourgeoisie'. It would have been easy enough for the translators to justify their use of this jargon word, if anyone had challenged them to do so. The warrant is Marx's own German. *Das Kapital* itself makes emphatic use of jargon, and even depends on jargon, at some of the most important moments of its argument.[4]

What is at stake in close attention to the letter of Marx's text? Is it, in fact, really to the 'letter' of the text that this observation on the word 'bourgeoisdom' suggests that we ought to pay attention? Are we not really thinking about the more complex and larger question of style? If we ask why Moore and Aveling (with Engels' editorial blessing) invented a jargon equivalent for the familiar German word *Bürgertum* when 'bourgeoisie' had existed in English for almost 200 years, is our question significant only for a narrow discussion of translation practice or is it a question about thinking in *Das Kapital* and thinking in *Capital*? How does Marx's own writing help us to answer this question?

In his report on the reception of the first edition of *Das Kapital*, Marx wrote that the 'Wortführer der deutschen Bourgeoisie'—literally, 'the spokesmen of the

German bourgeoisie' (F: 98) (Marx brushes them aside in the text of his preface with the mocking double epithet 'learned and unlearned', only in the next instant to savage them in a stylish footnote as 'breimäuligen Faselhänse', 'mealy-mouthed babblers' [F: 98–9; MA: 20; MEGA II.8: 52])—these world leaders in words, had berated the *style* of his book. Marx was sensitive to this criticism; or at least, he was sensitive to the possibility that its judgement of his book might be right, even if he was not disposed to feel vulnerable to the attacking performance of that judgement by the spokesmen of bourgeoisdom. 'No one,' he wrote, 'can feel the literary shortcomings [die literarischen Mängel] in *Capital* more strongly than I myself' (F: 99; MA 21; MEGA II.8: 52). Why should a critique of political economy be vulnerable, as Marx felt that Volume 1 of *Das Kapital* was vulnerable, to the accusation of literary shortcomings, and why should no one be able to feel these shortcomings more strongly than Marx? In his 1885 preface to the first edition of Volume 2 of *Das Kapital*, Engels describes the 'not finally polished' language of the notes by Marx that were left to him after Marx's death. They are in the 'language [. . .] in which Marx used to make his extracts: careless style full of colloquialisms, often containing coarsely humorous expressions and phrases interspersed with English and French technical terms'.[5] In his notes, at least, Marx enjoyed doing jargon in different voices. For Engels, as editor and compositor of Marx's great work, 'careless style' is a shortcoming in the obvious sense that it is the style of a text that was not finished by its author. But Volume 1 is a finished, 'polished' work when Marx comments painfully on its literary shortcomings. Where is the literary language in his book, and how is Marx measuring its importance? Is there in *Das Kapital* an implicit appeal not to a category of judgement belonging to its readers called 'aesthetic' judgement but to their variously and practically informed, variously and practically experienced, *taste* for literature?

Perhaps the most discriminating among the 'Faselhänse' or babblers will judge his shortcomings of style more justly than Marx himself ever could; but Marx says that no one judges those shortcomings more severely than he. It is important to understand what this means. It is nothing like a Lukácsian or Althusserian 'self-criticism'. Marx is not announcing to the readers of the second edition that he must retract a part of its former content or delete an incorrect tendency in his thinking. There is no disciplinarian monologue in which a quantity of ideology is detected in style, branded 'literary shortcomings' and then, in a staged confrontation with the Marxist faithful, confessed and eradicated. Marx's comment is, very consciously, a literary writer's expression of anguish over a failure of his own literary style that he recognizes but that he cannot simply emend. Why not? Because the failure he recognizes is a failure of style, and style is successful when it is intensifying and illuminating; language is not capable of being *emended* into intensity or into illumination.

These last words do not fit altogether easily into an account of Marx. Liebknecht could still sing, in 1896, as in the passionate tones of threnody, of Marx's 'burning love of freedom' that found 'expression in flaming, annihilating, elevating words';[6] but Lenin's critical and strategic disgust at the 'revolutionary phrase' soon afterward urged serious (that is, revolutionary) Marxists to resist the facile excitements of rhapsody, and innumerable mocking references to the rotten haloes and dazzling flaccid auras of poetic language made in common by authors as unlike as Trotsky and Mayakovsky might seem almost to prohibit the use of words like 'intensity' and 'illumination' in serious discussion of *Das Kapital*.[7] What really is the use of discussing the force of Marx's language as distinct from his theoretical propositions? Shouldn't Marx's comment about style be taken for a casual, pragmatic acknowledgement that he may have failed to put across his ideas as clearly as possible? What other failure of style could really matter to Marx besides the failure to make a theoretical proposition understood? The problem of style may in some measure be ineliminable from any attempt to write prose, we might admit; but do we not contrive to obscure more pressing theoretical problems when we too nicely or lingeringly dwell on it? Is all such dwelling really just aesthetic idling, poisonous to the impulse and capacity to think hard and clearly about real social relations, as Marx meant us to? Will it not always be at the *expense* of Marx's theory that we focus on his style, just as, in Goethe's and Schiller's view, it was at the *expense* of the spirit of Homer that philologists like Freidrich Wolf picked over the extant Homeric texts and concluded that they never 'flourished in the mouths of the Greeks' but that they had been 'altered, interpolated, corrected, and emended from the times of Solon down to those of the Alexandrians'?[8] Is philology, at the beginning of the twenty-first century as at the end of the eighteenth, in Marx's case as in Homer's, in competition with theory for the resources of intellectual loyalty?

Das Kapital is constructed in a way that suggests how readers should begin thinking about these questions. But it does require that anyone who thinks about them should be its reader: not simply the curator of its concepts. It is constructed from theoretical parts that are stylistically and methodologically distinct; it is written in styles that are clashing and disparate; some parts are more 'literary' than others. In his footnotes, for example, Marx clearly enjoys heightening the risk of style. The 'learned and unlearned' are, by their suppression into subscript, alchemically transfigured into mealy-mouthed drivellers, no longer merely savants who are wrong in theory but now the slaverers and swallowers of their knowledge, disgusting to the eye and ear. What does it mean that the first instance of direct satire against the *Kleinbürger*, the petty bourgeois, in *Das Kapital* occurs in a stylish footnote to a technical and apparently unambiguous discussion of relative forms of value? The *Kleinbürger*, anatomized in the filigree of subscript, sees in the production of commodities the 'Weltgipfel menschlicher Freiheit und individueller Unabhängigkeit', that is, in Moore and Aveling's *Capital*, 'the ne plus ultra of human freedom and individual independence', or in Fowkes' *Capital*, 'the absolute summit of human freedom and individual independence' (MEGA II.8: 98; MA: 79; F: 161). Why is this satirical portrait, an identification of bathos in the petty bourgeois worldview, done only in a footnote, and that, too, in a potentially distracting footnote to an important passage of economic exposition?[9]

The most conspicuously literary part of *Das Kapital*, in which, if anywhere, style is at explicit and significant risk of failure, is Part 1 of Volume 1. In particular, literary style is risked throughout the section of Part 1 called 'Der Fetischcharakter der Ware und sein Geheimnis', that is, the fetish-character of commodities and its secret (influentially mistranslated in both English versions as 'fetishism of commodities' and its secret, as if the translators had decided that Marx must have meant by 'fetishism' a mode of apprehending commodities, rather than, as Marx's word 'Fetischcharakter' more than suggests, a character belonging to commodities themselves). This most literary part of Marx's text is the part that Althusser commanded his French readers to regard as 'extremely harmful'.[10] *Das Kapital*, Althusser insists in his own preface to that text, is not, like that puerile and literary work *The German Ideology*, in essence a 'very ambiguous' book. *Das Kapital* is, and the workers must be made to understand that it is, 'a book of pure theory'.[11] In Althusser's view, there is, disastrously, jargon in Marx, particularly in the section on fetishism; but the real, that is, purely theoretical, Marx is never and categorically must not be in jargon. What Marx called 'literary shortcomings' are equivalent, on this view, to 'literature'—any trace and all of it. In the phantom, immaculately conceptual language that would be fit to do the work of Althusser's pure theory, the whole of style will be contamination. Karl Kautsky in his study of Marx's economic doctrines considered this most literary and stylish chapter on the fetish-character of commodities 'one of the most important in the book, to which every student ought to pay special attention';[12] but this is the same Kautsky later excommunicated by Lenin as a 'renegade', and recommendations of his sort can only strengthen the scientific

Marxist's resolve not to 'give way to literature' (to borrow a phrase from an author who used it because it was hilarious and insufferable).[13] Kautsky also judged, in 1887, that 'it is precisely this chapter which has been most neglected by the opponents, and even by the supporters, of the Marxian doctrines.'[14] If this was true in 1887, today the situation is the reverse. No part of *Capital* has received so much attention from literary theorists as Part 1, Section 4. Literary and cultural theory has made 'commodity fetishism' one of its central and most prodigal motifs. And yet, even those literary theorists apparently most sceptical or dismissive of the sort of puritanical disciplinary scaremongering found in Althusser's preface (and comparable essays in repression) have consistently treated—and still now do consistently treat—*Capital*, and Part 1, Section 4 in particular, almost or exactly as though it were 'pure theory'. Literary and cultural theorists have done this even when they have declared as a basic principle of its interpretation that *Capital* 'is not just constative, descriptive, truth-telling, but also performative, a speech act, a way of doing things with words'.[15] The merits and even the necessity of philology have been recited in homage to the literary qualities of Marx's writing but this same homage has tended to invoke philology only in order then to *justify the invocation* in theoretical terms rather than to reflect on the meaning of the text philologically.

I want in this chapter to suggest a number of reasons why *Capital* has been read, and is still now read, as pure theory, in ways that have in practice eliminated the problem of style from its interpretation, despite numerous attempts to insist on the significance of that problem and even to formulate it. I then want to discuss the style of *Capital* and the style of *Das Kapital*, and of Part 1, Section 4 in particular. I hope to demonstrate with this discussion, first, that Marx was not simply the theorist of capital and of social existence under capital, but also the author of an immensely daring and complicated *satire on social existence under capital*, and that his analysis of 'Der Fetischcharakter der Ware und sein Geheimnis' was, long before Guy Debord specified a conceptual meaning for the term, a work of sustained, aggressively satirical *détournement* in which risks and failures of style are arguments in themselves, irreducible to theoretical propositions;[16] and second, that resistance to philological interpretation of Marx among literary theorists, whether principled or unconscious, has contributed to a major misunderstanding of one of the most important ideas in *Das Kapital*.

SECOND TERM: *GALLERTE*

Conceived purely as a category of natural need, hunger
can be quenched with grasshoppers and gnat-cakes,
which many savages consume. But it is essential to the
concrete hunger of civilized people that they should
get something to eat which they do not find disgusting. In disgust and its opposite is reflected the whole
of history.

Theodor W. Adorno
'Theses on Need'[17]

The misunderstood idea in *Das Kapital* is the idea that 'abstrakt menschliche Arbeit' is a 'bloße Gallerte unterschiedsloser menschlicher Arbeit' (MEGA II.8: 70). One
reason why this idea in *Das Kapital* has been misunderstood by readers of *Capital* is that it is not present in *Capital*. Moore and Aveling translate Marx's phrase as 'human
labour in the abstract [...] a mere congelation of homogeneous human labour' (MA: 45). Fowkes writes 'human
labour in the abstract [...] merely congealed quantities of
homogeneous human labour' (F: 128). These are mistrans-
lations that cannot adequately be described as mere shortcomings in style; they significantly transform the meaning
of one of Marx's most important ideas *and the thinking that
it makes possible*. Why then are they accepted by readers of
Marx as though they did not transform his thinking?

Because, I will suggest, Marx has been read, and continues to be read, as though his thinking had nothing important to do with literariness and with style, or at least not in any radical sense. A little attrition of figurative or tonal particularity in the passage from text to commentary can be regarded as trivial from the perspective of 'pure theory' and its higher interpretive protocols. In other words, so long as Marx's concepts can be specified, Marx's style need only be enjoyed.

The most important way in which the meaning of Marx's thinking is transformed—not only by his translators but likewise, and as though collaboratively, by literary theorists—is through the elimination of satire from *Capital*. Ideas not merely expressed by Marx, but pressed by him inextricably into the thick of a complex satire intended for a complex and divided audience, are rescued from that pressure and paraphrased into a form fit for 'use' in Marxist cultural criticism. The elimination of satire is not obviously a conscious decision made by translators and theorists. More probably, it is negligence resulting from a rival solicitude. Commentary on 'abstract human labour' in the English translations of Marx and in literary theoretical interpretation of *Capital* is dominated by solicitude for concepts. Readers of Marx want to get the concepts exactly right. Commentary is dominated by that solicitude to the point where Marx's risks in style, his seizure, infiltration and parodic recycling of what he called 'the jargon of Political Economy', are not simply ignored, but programmatically decontextualized and obliviated.[18] The product is a text boiled down from its original state of internal generic disintegration, stripped of its difficult collage of the poetic, the scientific and the jargonistic *within individual sentences and ideas*, its constitutive ambiguity and, most important of all, its satire, and transformed into an array of undifferentiated concepts for theoretical consumption.

Capital does not include the idea, central to *Das Kapital*, that 'abstrakt menschliche Arbeit' is a 'bloße Gallerte unterschiedsloser menschlicher Arbeit'. It includes instead the substitute idea that 'human labour in the abstract' is 'a mere congelation of homogeneous human labour'. This substitute, imposed by Moore and Aveling and repeated by Fowkes, has the notable advantage that its conceptual content is easier to specify than the conceptual content of Marx's original phrase. Moore and Aveling's extremely influential account of abstract human labour is as follows. Human labour, described as having a single origin (it is 'homogeneous'), since we cannot see the multitude of its real origins in the commodities that are its products, is *frozen* in commodities: it is a 'congelation', from the Latin verb *congelare*, 'to freeze together', and the Latin noun *gelum*, 'frost'.[19] Human labour is abstract when it is frozen: lifeless, cold and immobilized. The

important word used in *Das Kapital* to describe the opposite condition of labour, that is, unabstract, living human
labour, must then be *flüssig*, flowing, as when Marx writes
that 'Menschliche Arbeitskraft im flüssigen Zustand oder
menschliche Arbeit bildet Wert, aber ist nicht Wert':
'[h]uman labour-power in motion, or human labour,
creates value, but is not itself value,' or '[h]uman labour-
power in its fluid state, or human labour, creates value, but
is not itself value' (MEGA II.8: 82; MA: 59; F: 142). This
use of *flüssig* in *Das Kapital* is no doubt significant, and it
is, of course, used by Marx to describe the lived experience of labour that is not present in 'abstract human
labour'.[20] But whereas *flüssig* is a direct antonym of 'congealed' and of 'frozen', it is not a direct antonym of the
word that Moore and Aveling and Fowkes translate as
'mere congelation' and as 'congealed quantities'. The word
they translate using the abstract noun 'congelation' is
Gallerte. *Gallerte* is not an abstract noun. *Gallerte* is now,
and was when Marx used it, the name not of a process like
freezing or coagulating but of a specific commodity.
Marx's German readers would not only have bought
Gallerte, they would have eaten it; and in using the name
of this particular commodity to describe not 'homogeneous' but, on the contrary, 'unterschiedslose', that is,
'undifferentiated' human labour, Marx's intention is not
simply to educate his readers but also to *disgust* them.

The image of human labour reduced to *Gallerte* is disgusting. *Gallerte* is not ice, the natural and primordial, solid and cold mass that can be transformed back into its original fluid condition by application of (e.g. human) warmth; *Gallerte* is a 'halbfeste, zitternde', that is, a 'semisolid, tremulous' comestible mass, inconvertible back into the 'meat, bone [and] connective tissue' of the various animals used indifferently to produce it. The sixth volume of the popular encyclopaedia *Meyers Konversations-Lexicon* (1888) gives the following entry:

> Gallerte (also *Gállert*, old German *galrat*, middle Latin *galatina*, Italian *gelatina*), the semisolid, tremulous mass gained from cooling a concentrated glue solution. All animal substances that yield glue when boiled can be used in the production of gallerte, that is to say, meat, bone, connective tissue, isinglass, stag horns, etc. It is easier to preserve gallerte by dissolving pure white glue (gelatine) in a sufficient quantity of water and letting it cool there. It is used in various dishes, *q.v.* jelly. Vegetable gallerte of lichen consists of lichen starch or algae slime and water. In particular it is prepared from Carragaheen, Icelandic moss and the like, and is often used, mixed with other medicaments, in medicine. Vegetable gallerte made of fleshy, sour fruits consists of pectins and water. Fruit jellies or jams are popular additions to other meals.[21]

The jargon in this entry overflows. *Gallerte* is the undifferentiated mess of glue-yielding 'tierischen Substanzen', animal substances industrially boiled down into condiments, that is, into 'Beigaben', 'additions' to meals rather than the staple nutrition of the meal itself. Marx says that 'abstract human labour', that is, both the units of human labour reduced to 'labour power' and wages in the calculations of the capitalist (calculations conducted in 'the jargon of Political Economy'), and human labour in general as 'value' expressed in commodities, is 'a mere *Gallerte* of undifferentiated human labour'. This 'mere *Gallerte*' is the product not of reversible freezing but of irreversible boiling followed by cooling. Abstract human labour is, in Marx's words, undifferentiated and *not* homogeneous, because it has a multitude of material origins (many workers contribute to the manufacture of each commodity, as political economy had recognized since Adam Smith's analysis of the division of labour in *The Wealth of Nations*),[22] but these multiple origins cannot be separately distinguished in the commodity which is the product of their combined activity. All that is meat melts into bone, and vice versa; and no effort of scrutiny, will or heated imagination, however powerfully analytic or moral, is capable of reversing the industrial process of that deliquescence.

It is important to recognize that this account of abstract human labour in *Das Kapital* is not just an isolated instance of merely graphic metonymy. Marx does not use the word *Gallerte* as mere literary flavouring to his theory, a delectable addition to the staple nutrition of concepts. It is not a word that can be separated from the sentence that accommodates it and enjoyed as style rather than specified as a concept. It cannot, because it changes the meaning of other passages in the text. It makes possible part of the thinking that happens later on in *Das Kapital*. What the image of human labour as *Gallerte* brings most forcefully to mind is not the antonymical word *flüssig* and its substratum of literary echoes in the metaphysical tradition of Heraclitus but another passage in *Das Kapital*, namely, the passage where Marx insists that labour is in reality a 'produktive Verausgabung von menschlichem Hirn, Muskel, Nerv, Hand, usw': 'a productive expenditure of human brains, muscles, nerves, hands, etc.' (MEGA II.8: 75; F: 134). This list, trailing off into a throwaway terminal expression, 'und so weiter', 'and so on', which Marx elsewhere habitually uses to abbreviate illustrative lists of commodities and raw materials, is two things at once. It is of course a materialist re-emphasis of the physical human experience at the origin of exchange value, that is, a labour theory of value; it is also, at the same time, a gruesome satirical echo of the allegorical account of abstract human labour as *Gallerte*. The living hands, brains, muscles and nerves of the wage labourer are mere 'animal substances', *ingredients* for the feast of the capitalist. The capitalist in turn is the great devourer of this undifferentiated human labour. He is not an individual, as Marx often repeats, but 'a mere embodiment of capital' (MA: 330). This satirical confinement of the capitalist to a personification not only makes him the oppressor of the workers in theory and in practice but also gives him a specific role in Marx's satire on consumption. The capitalist is roughly the industrial processing of the workers in reverse. The worker who starts out with a real body and brain is reduced to *Gallerte* by wage labour; and the capitalist who is in essence nothing but capital itself nonetheless assumes in his interactions with human beings the local habitation of a body and the name of an individual. This is what the worker and the capitalist are in Marx's satire on consumption, but Marx also says that this is what they are in reality, that is, in their 'real economic relation' of which all juridical relation 'is but the reflex' (MA: 96).

What is the status of satire in Marx? Satire is not an ornament. It is not the surplus of style decorating a substratum of conceptual content, just *Dichtung* supervening on *Wahrheit*. Satire and allegory are, to use Marx's words, 'phantoms formed in the human brain', but they are phantoms precisely as, and because, all theory and thinking are phantoms, pure theory no less than the most messily heterogeneous and undifferentiated.[23] Satire and allegory are also, 'necessarily', as Marx insists that phantoms in the brain must be, 'sublimates of [men's] material life process, which is empirically verifiable and bound to material premises'.[24] The opposition between phantom and material is a meaningful opposition in Marx but it is not the opposition between unreal and real, spirit and presence, or untruth and truth. It is a speculative opposition, which is to say that the distinction it makes is never conclusively attested in experience with anything like the force of apodicticity which pure theory might claim on its behalf. As Marx puts it, 'the characters who appear on the economic stage are but the personifications of the economical relations that exist between them' (MA: 97). The economic 'stage' is allegorical *and* real; it is where economical relations are both acted and lived. William Cowper's rebuke of overeloquent and artificial preachers who with 'histrionic mumm'ry [. . .] let down / The pulpit to the level of the stage' in *The Task* is, from the perspective of *Capital*, an instance of bourgeois ideology: the stage is not in reality the bathos of the pulpit; in reality, the pulpit was never anything but a prop on the stage.[25] What is capital in reality? It is profit on wage labour, and it is 'vampire thirst for the living blood of labour' (MA: 282). 'It must be acknowledged,' writes Marx, again invoking *Gallerte* and hinting ambiguously at an horrific euphemism, 'that our labourer comes out of the process of production other than he entered' (MA: 329–30).[26]

Gallerte is not only a specific commodity; on satire's terms, it is the *paradigmatic* commodity, the 'perfected non-world' of labour in a concentrated purchasable lump.[27] A lexicon of jargon trails after it. It is the tremulous edible product of industrial *reduction* and *processing*. This satire on the reduction of labour is not, for the following reason, further reducible to a mere concept. The difference between a concept and a satire is that satire is always, must always be, at someone's expense. All Marx's writing, and not just those moments in it that make economic theory overtly literary, is satirical in this sense. Marx always writes at someone's expense. Someone must be the object of satire and someone must suffer by its influence; and that means not simply that someone must be ridiculed or described grotesquely and with exaggeration but that the whole work of thinking in satire will be in the interests of some real people and contrary to the interests of others. From *Gargantua* to *Anti-Dühring*, *Peri Bathous* to the pompous scurrilities of Lacan's *Écrits*, thinking in satire is activated for one constituency of readers by its infliction on another. Satire in Marx is more than a comic modality of the picturesque: it is the concentrated literary exposure of social contradiction. It does not merely provide a comically distorted image of social reality but is in active conflict with social reality. Who suffers by Marx's account of abstract human labour, if it truly is a satire, and who is its object?

The worker reduced to *Gallerte* meets with the most horrible fate available in Marx's satire on wage labour but he is not for that reason the object of the satire. His suffering can hardly be increased by literature, and it is precisely in emphasis of this fact that Marx allocates to him the most repulsive fate in the drama. The worker's suffering is, for Marx, not just different in intensity but categorically different from the suffering of the bourgeoisie. The worker's suffering is not injured vanity, not displeasure at a grotesque image of himself, but 'dehumanization' and 'immiseration'. The object of Marx's satire on abstract human labour is not the worker reduced to a condiment but the bourgeois consumer who eats him for breakfast. It is the bourgeois consumer who suffers by the influence of Marx's satire on abstract human labour, because the satire makes his unavoidable daily acts and his very survival disgusting. What ought to be the fluid labour of living human beings is instead a disgusting, paradigmatically unnatural food product for the bourgeois consumer, the 'vampire which sucks out [the proletariat's] blood and brains and throws them into the alchemist's vessel of capital'.[28] But Marx, surely, is joking with his talk of vampires, and this, surely, is a book of theory before us, a 'critique of political economy', from whose scientific perspective the vampire must surely be an impossible person. No, Marx says in the *Communist Manifesto*, the point is that the vampire is not yet impossible, and it remains the task of revolution to see to it that he is 'made impossible'.[29] Its fetish-character may prevent the bourgeois consumer from seeing in *Gallerte* the brains, muscles, nerves and hands themselves; that is, the substance of the paradigmatic commodity may be undifferentiable back into its component human origins by any act of perception, however conscientious; but the bourgeois consumer who thus compulsorily worships the commodity as an idol is nonetheless cast by Marx's satire into the role of the child who daily begs to lick the cauldron clean, for refreshment, after daily observing the mess of human misery boil in it. Can the bourgeois consumer exit the stage of this satire, protesting his abstinence or his vegetarianism? No, he cannot, because the rendering of human minds and bodies into *Gallerte* is not, on the terms of Marx's satire, an abuse of wage labour by the coven of leading unreconstructed vampires but the fundamental law of all wage labour. The satire, just at the moment when its object might wriggle free of it, is revealed in fact to be 'theory'. The bourgeois object of satire is pinned to the fourth wall, since all his means of moral defence—his philanthropy, his austerity, his temperance—are, as he knows, incapable of making the slightest impression on a fundamental law: he is a great respecter of fundamental law, and so he is reduced to something like the transcendent impotence of the candidate for everlasting life in supplication of a God he secretly knows to be his own invention. Social existence under capitalism is thus gruesomely savage and primitivistic, not simply in that good bourgeois moderns behave toward commodities in the way that 'les anciens peuples [. . .] sauvages & grossiers' or 'les Noirs & les Caraïbes' of Enlightenment ethnography behaved toward their fetish idols[30] but in the still more disgusting sense that our most routine, unavoidable and everyday act, the act of consumption of use value—that is, first of all, purchase—is in every case an act of cannibalism.

Style is often regarded as something that must be got right, either in translation or in reading, so that a concept represented in it can be specified and then put to use in larger and more important analyses. But this care for the specification and use of concepts *after* style has been got right tends actually to diminish and enervate attention to style; attention to style is relegated into the warm-up for attention to concepts. The result, in literary theory, is, often enough, that style is got wrong in preparation for the theoretical use of the concepts represented in it. Marx's satire on wage labour as the fundamental savagery leading to compulsory everyday cannibalism is missed. We might say, more strongly still, that by getting style wrong, literary theory makes sure that it doesn't get style at all. Why should literary theory make sure that it doesn't get style in

Capital? In order to inoculate itself against what it wishes not to accept for its own proper object, that is, literature, as if to say that literature is an upstart object for imagining that it might have any claim to eminence among the universe of text materials available for interpretation. In the case of Marx's account of abstract human labour, this apparently democratic impulse to equalize the historical modalities of text in fact performs what Marx describes as the invariable work of bourgeois ideology: it occludes real social contradiction by reductively neutralizing satire into 'concepts'. Marx's account of abstract human labour is not only a theoretical indictment of bourgeois interests, it is also literature irreconcilable with the standard of truth and interpretation that is the reflex of those interests, to the extent that bourgeois readers are compelled, in order to make their own kind of sense of it, to separate its content from its style, to judge and contest the one and to enjoy or dislike the other, perhaps feeling that they in some sense stand accused by what Marx is saying but not seeing that his entire way of saying it is from start to finish, and unalterably, a satire at their own expense.

William Burroughs went far but not far enough. The point is not simply to make everyone see what is on the end of every fork, as the author of *Naked Lunch* described his purpose in publishing that undifferentiated mess of satirical fragments, but, more importantly, to make *you* see, as Kafka attempted, that no one but you could eat from the end of this fork, since the end of this fork was intended for you.

THIRD TERM: *FÉTICHISME*

> At five in the evening, the coast, which we kept always on our left, changed in aspect. The palm trees seemed to be in alignment with the shore, like the avenues with which French Châteaux are decorated: nature delighted thus in recalling the ideas of civilisation, in the very country where this civilisation was born and where, today, ignorance and barbarism reign.
>
> Chateaubriand
> 'Voyage d'Égypte'[31]

The concept of fetishism in *Das Kapital*, insofar as it is a concept, has its origin in Marx's reading and thinking about a French essay in theoretical ethnography published in 1760, Charles de Brosses's *Du Culte des Dieux Fétiches, ou Parallèle de l'ancienne Religion de l'Egypte avec la Religion actuelle de Nigritie*. This derivation of the concept of fetishism recycled in *Das Kapital* has been often noticed and reported as fact;[32] but astonishingly, the entire transmission of the concept out of De Brosses and into Marx has received no comment from Marx's literary theoretical interpreters. Marx's habit of misquoting famous authors in order to twist their language into a contradiction of its original meaning is well known. Goethe is *détourned* in a footnote mocking Proudhon, commodities are Shakespeare's Dame Quickly in reverse, and the preface to the first edition of 1867 is concluded with the high literary flourish of Dante *détourned*: 'Go on your own way, and let the people talk' in place of the original 'Follow me, and let the people talk' (F: 161, 93).[33] However well known this practice of Marx's may be, no commentator on Book 1, Section 4, 'Der Fetischcharakter der Ware und sein Geheimnis', has yet examined Marx's re-use of De Brosses's jargonistic neologism in the light of this practice or as an instance of it. No one, that is to say, has yet interpreted the concept of fetishism in *Capital* as a *détournement*. The passage of the term *fétichisme* from eighteenth-century aristocratic French into nineteenth-century communist German, and into Moore and Aveling's English; the violent resituation of the term out of ethnography which celebrates the enlightenment of European culture into a critique of political economy which seeks to expose that same culture's fundamental injustice; the implicit satire, not simply against superstitious thinking and behaviour but also against the centuries-long continuity of bourgeois civilized disgust at 'superstition' itself, activated by the reappearance of the term in a context for which it was not originally fitted; the whole involuted literary and satirical structure of Marx's *re-use* of the concept has been routinely ignored, as though *Capital* straightforwardly invited its readers to extract from it something called 'the theory of commodity fetishism'. Each time this theory is extracted, the impurities of style and satire are washed away with the caustic of 'pure theoretical' paraphrase.

Althusser is not merely the most egregious culprit. He is the unacknowledged legislator of the majority of literary theoretical readings produced in the spirit of pure theory. When Althusser insists on 'the necessity of reading Marx's text *very closely*', his text becomes an exhibition of Freudian *Verleugnung* or disavowal in reverse: the adamant *avowal* of 'reading', pushed at us in overtly pedagogical commands, conceals the real, underlying *disavowal* of reading in his interpretation of *Capital*.[34] Althusser's emphatic disciplinarianism—Read *very closely*!—echoes an instance of Lenin's. 'It is impossible completely to understand *Capital*,' Lenin infamously wrote, 'without having thoroughly studied and understood the *whole* of Hegel's *Logic*.'[35] For Althusser, it is not only possible, but imperative, to completely understand *Capital*. On these terms, the interpretation of Marx becomes inimical to 'reading' Marx the moment interpretation imports any problem or difficulty of its own into the work of pure theoretical comprehension.

Literary and cultural theorists who might disavow this purgation of 'reading' nonetheless often do not transgress its rule that *Capital*, including the section on the fetish-character of the commodity, be read as pure theory. A representative treatment, more subtle than Althusser's but innocent of any transgression of his rule, is this by Laura Mulvey:

> The Marxist concept [of fetishism] is derived from a problem of inscription: that is, the way in which the sign of value is, or rather fails to be, marked onto an object, a commodity. It is in and around the difficulty of signifying value that commodity fetishism flourishes.[36]

Mulvey's account is similar to the majority of accounts now current.[37] Fetishism in Marx is a concept, the concept is derived from a problem, and the problem is a conceptual one. Commodity fetishism then flourishes in and around a conceptual problem. Sticking to Mulvey's own terms, we might ask: If the inscription of value, or rather of 'the sign of value', has already failed, how can anyone be blamed for not reading that inscription? Already the expenses of satire are discounted. There is nothing disgusting about failing to read the already failed inscription of a sign of value onto an object. Nothing could be more innocently remote from the murder, cannibalism and idol worship of savages than epistemological perplexity over

54

the vicissitudes of signification. If this is the fetishism we practice, we have nothing to worry about, however much we may have to speculate on. But we cannot take Mulvey's account of Marx on its own terms because it completely excludes from view the most important fact about the 'concept' of fetishism in *Capital*, namely, that it is a satirical concept, insofar as it is a concept at all, and that it is derived not from reflection on abstract problems of inscription but from Marx's ironic reading and *détournement* of an eighteenth-century essay in racist ethnography. Mulvey both excludes philological thinking from her own reflections on Marx and ignores the philological work done by *Capital* itself.

The exclusion is good for theoretical efficiency. With all trace of philology excluded from the theoretical equation, fetishism is a concept and *Capital* is theory. Besides being a one-sided and impoverished description of Marx's writing and thinking, the definition of fetishism as a practice that flourishes 'in and around the difficulty of signifying value' leads to a vision of problem-solving (a more subtle practice than revolution, and more bloodless) that any vampire would find deliciously sanguine. 'For Marx', writes Mulvey,

> the value of a commodity resides in the labor power of its producer. If this labor power could ever inscribe itself indexically on the commodity it produces, if it

> could leave a tangible mark of the time and skill taken
> in production, there would be no problem.[38]

No problem of what kind? Are we meant to conclude that the bourgeois consumer is a fetishist because labour power fails to inscribe itself indexically on its object? Is it the inaptitude of labour power for acts of indexical inscription that makes the bourgeois consumer merely resemble a cannibal? No, because in the rarefied atmosphere of pure theoretical interpretation, sanitized of any reference to Marx's satire, his literary allegory and his aggression, there is no room for the word 'bourgeois' in the sense that Marx meant it. 'Bourgeois' itself becomes jargon, an item of diction belonging to a superannuated political attitude, a verbal embarrassment; and rather than examining how pure theory itself contributes to this jargonization of revolutionary language through its discountenance of satire, the practitioners of pure theory instead imagine that the jargonization was already long ago complete (or 'always already' was complete) and that their own delicate avoidance of revolutionary language is a testimony to theoretical sobriety and realism. The failures of indexicality may yet turn out to be someone's fault, in some just about imaginable appendix to the analysis of the signification of value; but it seems unlikely, because that analysis is constructed without reference to the possibility that Marx's whole account of the practice of fetishism is unalterably at someone's expense, and that the description of fetishism in *Capital* is a satire irreconcilable with the standards of truth maintained in the interests of bourgeois realism. *Capital* is processed into a book of pure theory. Drop the satire and no one gets hurt.

Marx's thinking in *Capital* is philological as well as satirical, just as the risks of style in his satire are themselves the work of thinking and not a mere decoration of thinking. To understand what Marx means by the fetish-character of commodities, and why fetishism in *Capital* is at best only ambiguously a 'concept', we need to reconstruct the literary composition of his chapter, paying close attention to its satirical transformations of its literary source material; and we need to ask at whose expense the theory is written, and what kind of expense Marx meant to inflict by it.

De Brosses was the first writer to use the word *fétichisme*, a word that his first readers must surely have thought jargonistic, and his long essay offers the first theoretical commentary on it.[39] His essay cannot be made to qualify on Althusserian terms as 'pure theory'. Giorgio Agamben's criticism of De Brosses, that his 'astonishment [. . .] before the fetish not only has no reason to exist, it betrays a forgetfulness of the original status of objects', is a good example of how the attempt to read *Du Culte des Dieux Fétiches* as pure theory ends up occluding what is most characteristic and important about the essay.[40] Throughout the essay De Brosses protests on behalf of his own constituency of enlightened moderns, that is, the sane and mature, monotheistic European intellectuals capable of abstract reasoning (not the vulgar working people of 1760), that 'one cannot prevent oneself from being astonished by the fact that nations and ages [siècles] so remote from each other should agree on the same idea' (that is, the idea that inanimate objects and animals should be worshipped).[41] This insistence of irresistible astonishment recurs throughout the essay. Both the *disgusting* phenomenon of fetish worship itself, and the global and transhistorical epidemic of its practice, spanning the centuries and the continents from ancient Egypt to the present-day 'nation' of Africa, are irresistibly astonishing to anyone disciplined by the practice of rational inquiry into the causes of appearances.[42] The astonishment which Agamben, in a gesture of Heideggerian reproof, dismisses as 'forgetfulness of the original status of objects', is for De Brosses not simply a comportment of *Dasein* before the ontic, remediable by an act of phenomenological remembrance but a form of polite, literary socializing among equals, a way of dramatizing and giving confessional literary colour to his recognition of the kindred intelligence of his readers.[43] We, gentlemen readers, must irresistibly be astonished by the practices of savages, since only our elaborately literary astonishment, most emphatically performed (and not any straight ethnographic empiricism, had anything of the sort been imaginable in 1760) will give proof that our difference from savages is by now an intellectually and morally categorical difference and not a difference merely of degree. The practice of literary astonishment is *irresistible* in the sense that it fulfils a moral imperative and serves as evidence of a civilized sensibility. *Judge then of my astonishment* is the conventional English invitation that flourished in the late eighteenth and nineteenth centuries. It is the reaction of the sensitive, civilized inquirer, innocent of perversity, confronted by some extravagance that gives him the chance to establish sympathetic mutuality with his readers on the grounds of their common difference from the stupid and the unenlightened. The attitude, that is, which Beckett parodies in the figure of the divinely appointed inquirer Jacques Moran, astonished by the impertinence of his pubescent idiot son in *Molloy*. Whatever we might think is its psychogenesis or its significance for a theory of object relations, De Brosses's astonishment before the practice of fetish worship was then, and is now, an irreducibly literary and conversational astonishment. It may ambiguously be good material for a symptomatology of enlightenment; but for Marx it was, first of all, unambiguously good material for a satire on the conventional literary means of establishing defensive moral mutuality among aristocrats. De Brosses's astonishment is the artificial testimony of the author's involuntary reflex, a moral reaction to barbarism, and the sympathy of his readers will be all the more readily forthcoming since it will function to consolidate in their minds 'l'accord unanime des hommes intelligens & des nations éclairés': 'the unanimous agreement of intelligent men and enlightened nations'.[44]

De Brosses is of course not content simply to remain paralyzed in this attitude of polite astonishment, like some *homme sauvage* paralyzed in superstitious reverence under a snake or a wooden idol 'forged by the excess of his stupidity'.[45] The drama of literary astonishment must involve a second act. De Brosses will collect himself and recover wit enough to propose a theoretical account of why fetishism has been and is still an indigenous practice in otherwise widely contrasting and historically unconnected cultures.

> When one sees similar practices among men living in ages and in climates so far removed from each other, who have nothing in common besides their ignorance and their barbarism, it is still more natural to conclude that man is made this way; that for man left in his rough and savage natural state, unformed and uninstructed by imitation, primitive morals and the means of production [les façons de faire] are the same in Egypt as in the Antilles, the same in Persia as among the Gauls: everywhere the same mechanism of ideas,

from which the same actions follow. And if one is surprised by this particular point, which indeed seems
very strange; if one is astonished to see fetishism widespread among all the uncultivated peoples [les peuples
grossiers] of the universe, and in all times, and in all
places; to explain this phenomenon one need only recollect the proper cause of it already cited: it is the constant uniformity of the savage man with himself; his
heart exposed perpetually to fear, his soul greedy without pause for hope, deliver up his ideas to error and
deviation and carry him off into a thousand acts de-
void of sense; his mind, without culture and without
reasoning, is incapable of apperceiving the little that it
finds of the connection between causes and the effects
that wait on them. Since no one is astonished to see
children fail to elevate their minds above their dolls,
to see them believing that their dolls are animate
and acting with them accordingly, why should he be
astonished to see people whose life passes in continual
infancy, and who are never more than four years of age,
reason without the least accuracy, and act according to
how they reason? Minds of this calibre are the most
common, even in the ages of enlightenment and
among the civilized nations.[46]

Literary astonishment is, in De Brosses, the conventional
prologue to theoretical illumination. *If one is astonished*
(and one must be astonished, since the enormity of the
facts is irresistibly astonishing), *one need only recollect*.
Theoretical illumination is the recollection of what is

natural and manifest but tends in practice to be forgotten or overlooked. What the scheduled recovery of wit after astonishment in this case establishes is that *les peuples grossiers* are, of course, familiar to us after all, because they are infants. The drama of astonishment is De Brosses's. He is at once its enlightened author and the protagonist of its comic action. The infant cannibals of the universe have a specific part to play in the noble comedy of De Brosses: they are the monsters who are domesticated through De Brosses's sympathetic disciplining of his own astonishment with the cool instrument of theoretical reason. Once the 'liaison entre causes & effets' is heroically restored to view by our ethnographer protagonist, the comic bewilderment of misidentifications and cross-nakedness is all resolved, and there, in the limelight of theoretical illumination, standing before us, before the audience of mutual sympathizers, is the monster unmasked—it is our own child, tenderly observed from above, prattling at its toys in a paradise of innocence![47]

Fetishism in *Du Culte des Dieux Fétiches* is not a 'concept'; it is, rather, the subject of a drama. The drama depends on a specific historical dramatis personae sharing specific relations. The luminary astonished by the cannibal does not *remain* astonished: the action and coherence of the drama require that he should discipline his astonishment and rescue the cannibal. Like a kiss on a frog, theory turns the ugly cannibal back into a loveable child, rescuing universalism. The second act of ethnographic inquiry, *after* the confession of moral astonishment, is to put in place the 'liaison entre causes & effets' even and precisely in those circumstances apparently most uncongenial to rational thinking: the *mise en scène* of comic bewilderment and misidentification. What this literary practice of astonishment and discipline creates and depends on is the image of the absolutely stupefied individual, which it then satirically dominates as the specimen subject of its work of curative theoretical diagnosis. The figure of the absolutely stupefied individual is conceived in the drama of literary astonishment and its theoretical disciplining; and the stupefaction of this figure can then be defined, in part circularly, as his inability to act out that same drama in the role of its protagonist, his lifelong confinement to a cameo, in other words, the incapacity of the savage for ethnographic astonishment at what is imperatively astonishing, and his inability to discipline the astonishment he cannot feel. This is the ethnographic negative mirror image instituted by the drama of astonishment and its disciplining. The practice of illumination defines itself through literary and theoretical definition of the absolutely stupefied figure who is incapable of it. The ethnographer establishes his own maturity, Kant's famous *Mündigkeit*, the condition of intellect necessary for autonomous life, through his diagnosis of the infantilism of barbarians.[48] The whole drama is thus a satire, ostensibly at the expense of a barbarian figure that modern ethnography would dismiss as a figment, but covertly at the expense of still infantile moderns whose lightly distorted image is locked in that figment as in an obligatory cameo. The drama is a satirical exercise in establishing sympathetic mutuality between members of the same class. As the French scholar M. V. David has commented, 'One mustn't forget that *Dieux fétiches* is not merely a learned work, but also an innovative and polemical work.'[49] Not, that is, merely a theory of fetish worship but a stylish attack on the commonalty of fetishists who are still the majority in 'the ages of enlightenment and among the civilized nations'.

Slavoj Žižek is one of the few theorist commentators on Marx's concept of fetishism to offer a brief discussion of De Brosses's essay.[50] His interpretation of *fétichisme* in De Brosses might seem to be saying something similar to what I have said about the drama of literary astonishment and theoretical disciplining. But there is a significant difference between Žižek's account and mine. Žižek writes:

> The notional background for fetishism [. . .] lies in evolutionist universalism: 'fetishism' has a place within the notion of a universal human history progressing

> from the lower stage (the veneration of natural
> objects) to the abstract spiritualized stage (the purely
> spiritual God); it allows us to grasp the unity of
> human species, to recognize the Other, while none
> the less asserting our superiority. The fetishist Other
> is always 'lower'—that is to say, the notion of fetishism
> is strictly correlative to the gaze of the observer
> who approaches the 'primitive' community from the
> outside.[51]

This seems on the face of it to be something like the point
I'm making. I argued that the figure of the absolutely stupefied individual or savage is conjured by De Brosses in a
drama of literary astonishment and theoretical disciplining. This figure is not in my reading, however, the same
thing as Žižek's 'fetishist Other', and is not exchangeable
for him because he is not in De Brosses's essay the product of 'the gaze of the observer'; he is, rather, the product
of a satirical literary conversation. Žižek's fetishist is not a
dramatis persona but a psychic projection. His appearance
is not made, as the appearance of the figure of the absolutely stupefied individual is made, in the *mise en scène* of
literary writing seeking to establish sympathetic mutuality with readers of a specific class; his appearance is fabri-
cated by 'us' when we 'recognize the Other, while none
the less asserting our superiority'. In other words, Žižek's
interpretation of De Brosses's 'fetishist' is psychoanalytic,
not literary, and his account of the fabrication of the image

of the fetishist is a theoretical account of how 'our superiority' is asserted. Žižek is reading De Brosses not as literature in conversation with a specific historical class, but as evidence or material for a generalized psychoanalytic account of the mechanisms of narcissism. Philology on hold, *Du Culte des Dieux Fétiches* is processed into material for pure theory.

When Žižek moves on in his argument from De Brosses to Marx, the only transmission of the concept of fetishism visible to his gaze is a pure theoretical transmission. The language of De Brosses's essay is nowhere mentioned or implicated, and there is no consideration nor even a recognition of the fact that Marx *read* an antiquated and objectionable, racist and aristocratic, unscientifically ethnographic essay called *Du Culte des Dieux Fétiches*.[52] Žižek's only direct question, similar to Mulvey's, is how Marx and Freud displace 'the notion of fetishism' from its previous anthropological use.[53] My point is that Marx did not displace a notion. He wrote a stylish and satirical *détournement*, not simply of the word *fétichisme* or of the concept of *fétichisme* in De Brosses but of the whole drama of literary astonishment and sympathetic theoretical disciplining in which the figure of the absolutely stupefied individual in De Brosses is conjured. Unlike Žižek, Marx read De Brosses as literature. His chapter on the fetish-character of commodities is a satirical exploitation of the literary shortcomings of De Brosses, a communist speculation on the production of an aristocrat.

Marx plunges us into astonishment at the beginning of his analysis of the fetish-character of commodities in a moment of stylistic transition that is very abrupt and dramatic. We pass from a table illustrating the money form and a number of abstract illustrations of value equivalence in algebraic expressions, directly into the famous first sentences of Part 1, Section 4:

> Eine Waare scheint auf den ersten Blick ein selbstverständliches, triviales Ding. Ihre Analyse ergiebt, daß sie ein sehr vertracktes Ding ist, voll metaphysischer Spitzfindigkeit und theologischer Mucken (MEGA II.8: 100).

> A commodity appears, at first sight, a very trivial thing, and easily understood. Its analysis shows that it is, in reality, a very queer thing, abounding in metaphysical subtleties and theological niceties (MA: 81).

Our delivery into astonishment comes not at first glance but at second. Or rather, there is no second glance (*Blick*), since the second act of perception in this satirical doubletake is already an act of 'analysis'. The drama of astonishment and discipline played out in De Brosses is enlarged at a stroke: astonishment is no longer the comedy of misidentification which sets the stage for the moment of reconciliation with nature accomplished by theoretical reason; astonishment now belongs to theoretical reason itself. Astonishment is not the prologue to reason but the achievement of reason. We are astonished only when we do the work of analysis; not before. The *mise en scène* of comic bewilderment in *Das Kapital* is not our astonishment but our confidence. We think we understand very well what commodities are but this confidence is nothing but the vanity of a dramatis persona given to incessant acts of comic misidentification. Commodities are obvious, self-explanatory, trivial and everyday objects, we tell ourselves in the first act, just as for Diderot's Jacques the fatalist every event, however unexpected or unintelligible, is obviously just the everyday workings of destiny and providence 'écrit là-haut', 'written up above'.

The stage is set, in this prologue to theoretical disillumination, for a literary conversation that will illuminate sympathetic mutuality between Marx and his readers by pointing its analysis at the dupes of universal confidence. All that needs to be established is that the person incapable of astonishing himself through an analysis of commodities is an infant, or a barbarian, or a cannibal; in any case that whatever kind of fairy or monster this person might be, he is *not us*. But that comfortable and sympathetic reality is denied in the space of a sentence; in fact, it is conjured by Marx *so that* it may be denied. Marx does not simply deny that the commodity is a self-explanatory object. He also, just as significantly, denies that we can expect on the basis of this denial itself to enjoy sympathetic mutuality as readers of his work. A sympathetic literary conversation is conjured and rejected. We who are the readers of this book will not be its Olympian diagnosticians (theorists of the sign, psychoanalysts, ethnographers, moralists) but are ourselves the subject specimens of its diagnosis. Mutual apprehension of the commodity, this 'very strange thing' (F: 163), if possible at all, would require from us not a glance but a universal analysis; and to defeat that possibility we are told immediately that the analysis required will bring to light a wildly unfamiliar and recondite image of the commodity, an image that is, first of all, so complex and daunting that only the professional thinker will be able to comprehend it, an image that is in fact so astonishing, so abundantly metaphysical and theological, that no imaginable act of theoretical disciplining can be expected to advance us out of the astonishment it causes. We will not be reconciled to this strange thing, it will not be shepherded by our common sense into the limelight of conclusive theoretical illumination, and if we are the protagonist of this drama of unexitable astonishment and impossible discipline it is on the basis that our act of heroic resolution is scheduled to take place offstage at some moment after the drama has finished.[54] We will not be the person who performs that act, because the person is impossible; we are instead the person, like the infant vampire who licks clean the cauldron of *Gallerte*, sucking the blood off his milk teeth, who is real by negative virtue of not yet being impossible. On this basis, not on the basis of our comic sympathies and delusory confidences, we are invited to proceed into Mr Marx's arcane disquisition on the 'secret' of the commodity.

Marx's readers as invited into the drama of *Capital* are not, as De Brosses's readers are, the companions of the author and the sympathetic participants in his enlightened conversation. Demystification of the commodity in *Capital* is aggressively satiric: we grow up beyond the Kantian 'self-imposed immaturity' of unthinking confidence, we leave a phantom home on the promise of a material home, only to be lodged by analysis itself in a mysterium more nauseatingly intricate and Byzantine than anything in the phantom playground we were so proud to grow out of. 'The religious reflex of the real world,' Marx tells us in the course of his analysis, 'can, in any case, only then finally vanish, when the practical relations of everyday life offer to man none but perfectly intelligible and reasonable relations with regard to his fellow men and to nature' (MA: 91–2). Whereas 'analysis' might be expected to bring us a little closer, at least, to the 'real world' in whose reflex Marx tells us we are incarcerated, just as it does for De Brosses; and whereas we might in theory expect that our relations should become just a little more 'intelligible and reasonable', if not yet 'perfectly' so, through our practice of analysis, since, after all, analysis is nothing if not the application of intelligence and reason; as it turns out, we are taught by Marx that no approach of this sort will be made by us, that analysis of our world will remain impassable astonishment at it because *we ourselves are the condition of impossibility* of 'perfectly intelligible and reasonable relations'. Why then should analysis be attempted, if the practice of it amounts in this way not only to a confirmation of the impotence of the intellectual aspiration to virtue and *Mündigkeit* but also to an active deepening of that impotence, even to the point of despair? (In another form, this will be my question in Chapter 2.) The commodity, we are astonished to discover, is 'transubstantiation' and 'metamorphosis', its analysis conducted by the historical materialist Karl Marx in the jargon of Catholic mysteries and ancient myth. We knew this language was jargon before reading *Das Kapital*; and, equipped with our knowledge that it is jargon, we had been able to reject the use and the authority of it. Now we are told that our analysis of 'metaphysical' commodities must indulge this same old language, still as much a jargon as ever, but this time, we might think, a jargon repeated as farce with us readers as its hilariously masked and unmasked clowns and rustics. Why must we?

The answer to that question is that the section on the fetish-character of commodities in *Das Kapital* is a satire at the expense of the readers I have been calling 'us'. The readers I have been calling 'us' are bourgeois readers. The drama of anguished response to Marx's *détournement* of the function of 'analysis' that I just now acted out is anticipated by *Das Kapital*, whose satiric expectation is that readers locked into that internal monologue of objections and bewilderment will on instinct revert to mere theoretical mastery over it. This is what bourgeois readers do. The instinct to theoretical mastery of concepts is a class instinct. They may not deny that the state of affairs described by Marx is in some sense their own fault, at least on Marx's own terms; but they will find the imputation of direct personal culpability to be, in theoretical terms, a dead end, all anger and no insight, merely an invitation to intellectual claustrophobia and sanctimonious gestures of abstract repentance; and so, to grow out of that dead end by discountenancing it, they will make use of Marx's 'concepts' as though those concepts were, for theoretical thinkers, the important meaning in *Capital*, extricable *in toto* from the mess of satirical accusation and prophylactic analysis and, not *re-usable*, but usable with impressive originality in any new context of criticism whatever, from the criticism of fallibility in indexical sign-inscription to the criticism of 'presence in general'.[55] In his recent essay on fetishism in Marx, Jean-Luc Nancy writes:

> Behind the unveiled secret, another more convoluted
> secret cloaks itself—one that perhaps will never be re-
> vealed absolutely: it is that of presence in general,
> which might never be exempt of fetishism, that is, of
> the force of the desire by which I reach toward this
> presence in order to see it, touch it, and savor it, at least
> from the moment that 'presence' does not designate
> the inert being of what has been put there (what has
> been placed there) and which is not even *there*, nor
> there, nor beyond, no matter where it is placed.[56]

The discountenancing of dead-end criticism in favour of open-ended thaumaturgy is one among many trends in bourgeois theoretical mastery over the concepts of *Das Kapital*, one among many ways that a bourgeois reader can discount the personal expenses of Marx's satire against him. What this passage by Nancy does (which lots of other theoretical trends also do) is to discover, 'behind' the problem dramatized by Marx, some other, more primordial problem, some 'convoluted' dimension of the problematic itself which proves all the more amenable to an exclusively theoretical treatment the more interestingly it can be imagined to resist revealing itself. Nancy frees theory from the expenses of satire in the same tradition as Heidegger, the long tradition of commentary on Heraclitus' aphorism *phusis kruptesthai philei*, 'nature loves to hide'.[7] But theorist authors who claim loyalty to altogether different trends make what amounts to the same move. Thus Žižek:

> Beneath the apparently humanist–ideological opposi-
> tion between 'human beings' and 'things' lurks another,
> much more productive notion, that of the mystery of
> substitution and/or displacement: how is it ontologi-
> cally possible that the innermost 'relations between
> people' can be displaced on to (or substituted by)
> 'relations between things'?[58]

How is it possible? For theory that is interested only in
the theory in *Das Kapital*, it is possible by theoretical fiat.
As Derrida liked to say, 'Why not?' 'Whether questions
are essential,' wrote Adorno, 'can only be judged by the
answers given.'[59] There is perhaps a dimension of the
problematic that is transcendentally amenable to pure theory, a dimension in which the most *perfectly* intelligible
and reasonable questions are those which cost so little to
ask that the challenge for thinking becomes not to answer
them but to ask them with such enormous prodigality and
largesse in the management of concepts that their unit
cost within the economy of theoretical interrogation is
finally reduced to nil. (In a different form, this is my subject in Chapter 3.)

The fetish-character of commodities described by
Marx is truly an intellectual dead end. It does cramp the
reader into a gesture of abstract repentance that cannot be
other than sanctimonious. This compression is its satire,
the literary thinking that declares that its standard of
truth is irreconcilable with the bourgeois expectation that

astonishment will be disciplined into recollection of the natural and manifest. *Das Kapital détourns* not just the jargon of *Du Culte des Dieux Fétiches* but its whole satiric drama of sympathetic mutuality and rescue; and it blocks the reductive processing of its *détournement* into an array of concepts to be held at the disposal of theory by anticipating that this is what bourgeois readers will want to do with it. Any interpretation of Marx that forgets the dramatis persona of the bourgeois reader, who is, of course, living and real, that passes over him in silence, or that conjures some elaborate theoretical periphrasis to occupy his place more interestingly than he can, is a complacent misinterpretation to the full extent that it discounts the fundamental expense of Marx's satire. That expense is not a concept in *Das Kapital*; it is the lived, practical infliction of the text on intelligent readers who may reject the jargon of 'transsubstantiation' in its Catholic use just as they will reject its 'joking' use in Marx's analysis of the commodity, but who continue, 'unthinkingly' or not, to eat human beings transubstantiated by industrial reduction into the base of *Gallerte* in every single commodity on the market.

It hardly needs to be said, I hope, that in arguing that Marx is satire, *détournement*, drama and jargon, I am in no way saying or allowing that *Das Kapital* is 'not true'. What I am saying is that the practice of truth in *Das Kapital* is a spectrum extending from the absolutely literal to the irreducibly satiric, and that this spectrum of truth is reduced to an undifferentiated, tremulous and semisolid mass of more easily swallowed veracity by pure theoretical accounts of Marx that are too intelligently claustrophobic to inhabit the dead end of a terminal and perfected contradiction. Despite all the discounts theoretically on offer, this contradiction in reality persists: it is as terminal right now as it was in 1867. Bourgeois reader, this dead end is intended for you.

Notes

This essay was published in *World Picture* 1 (2008) and is reprinted here with the journal's permission.

1. Wilhelm Liebknecht, *Karl Marx: Biographical Memoirs* (E. Untermann trans.) (London: The Journeyman Press, 1975), p. 75. Cf. Turgot, *Turgot: Textes choisies et préface* (Pierre Vigreux ed.) (Paris: Dalloz, 1947), p. 60, where Turgot's editor makes the identical claim about the prose of a rival political economy: 'It has been said with good reason that *the style is the man himself* [*le style est l'homme même*]. Turgot's style is particularly characteristic' (my translation).

2. The phrase is John Henry Newman's from his famous letter to Charles Kingsley of 17 January 1864. John Henry Newman, *Apologia Pro Vita Sua* (Ian Ker ed.) (London: Penguin: 2004), p. 368.

3. Karl Marx, *Capital* (Friedrich Engels ed., Samuel Moore and Edward Aveling trans.) (New York: Modern Library, 1936[1886]), pp. 25–6; Karl Marx, *Capital* (Ben Fowkes trans.) (London: Penguin, 1990 [1976]), p. 103. Throughout this chapter I adopt the following convention for referring to three texts of Volume 1 of *Das Kapital*: 'MA' for *Capital* (Samuel Moore and Edward Aveling trans.); 'F' for *Capital* (Ben Fowkes trans.); 'MEGA II.8' for *Das Kapital* [2nd German edn, 1872] in *Marx-Engels-Gesamtausgabe*, VOL. 2.8 (Berlin: Dietz, 1989 [1975]). Further references to these three texts appear in parentheses.

4. Marx was never anything like a straightforward despiser of jargon but always regarded jargon as one language material among many, equally capable of conscious and unconscious as well as of effective and ineffective use. In other words, Marx's attitude to jargon in general was never simply contemptuous; often his attitude was artistic, playful and literary. The puritanical rejection of jargon as corrupt language unreusable in serious argument is from Marx's perspective pompous and undialectical. One of Marx's scornful observations on 'Critical Criticism' at the beginning of *The Holy Family* is that 'it scorns writing for experts, it writes for the general public, banning all outlandish expressions, all "Latin intricacies, all professional jargon".' [Karl Marx and Friedrich Engels, *The Holy Family, or a Critique of Critical Criticism: Against Bruno Bauer and Company* (Richard Dixon and Clemens Dutt trans.), in *Collected Works*, VOL. 4

(London: Lawrence and Wishart, 1975), p. 9]. Among the unfinished notes for Volume 2 of *Das Kapital*, written in what Engels called Marx's 'careless style', there is an ironic reference to 'the jargon of Political Economy' [Karl Marx, *Capital*, VOL. 2 (London: Lawrence and Wishart, 1986), p. 223]. The reference is ironic because Marx refers with this phrase to the everyday language of capitalist employment practices and not to any specialized vocabulary beyond the reach of factory workers. Marx had enough respect for his readers not to imagine that they needed protecting from recondite diction and erudite allusions; he also had enough contempt for them to relish imagining their discomfort over the same diction and allusions.

5. Ibid., p. 1.

6. Liebknecht, *Biographical Memoirs*, p. 76.

7. Criticism of 'poetic' language by Marxists usually amounts to an excursus from the more central criticism of 'idealism'. It is a criticism dominated by a particular tradition of Marxist polemic, the fighting rhetoric of Bolshevik anti-Platonism. See, for example, Nikolai Bukharin, *Philosophical Arabesques* (Renfrey Clarke trans.) (New York: Monthly Review Press, 2005), p. 245: '[T]here will be no room for the hypertrophy of the "spiritual", under the influence of which the object evaporated, as it were, being transformed (not in reality, of course, but in the heads of philosophers) into an "idea", a "concept", or some other emaciated, cachetic abstraction located on the upper contours of thought.' This even as

Bukharin was in prison awaiting his last show trial, a *locus amoenus* with a notable history of prompting exactly the consolations of antimaterialist philosophy which Bukharin scornfully and conventionally rejects. Cf. Surrey's poem on his incarceration in the Tower of London, 'The stormes are past, these cloudes are overblowne', and line 8 in particular, where the hypertrophy of spirituality within the prisoner is set against the atrophy of freedom in the world at large, according to the convention of Boethian consolation: 'Thraldom at large hath made this prison fre' [Henry Howard, Earl of Surrey, *Poems* (Emrys Jones ed.) (Oxford: Clarendon, 1964), p. 33].

8. F. A. Wolf, *Prolegomena to Homer* (Anthony Grafton, Glenn W. Most and James E. G. Zetzel trans.) (Princeton: Princeton University Press, 1985), p. 209. Goethe's riposte, in which he berates Wolf for turning Homer into a 'patchwork', is his poem 'Homer wieder Homer' ('Homer versus Homer'). Johann Wolfgang von Goethe, *Sämtliche Werke* (Gisela Henckmann and Irmela Schneider eds), VOL. 13.1 (München: Carl Hanser Verlag, 1992), p. 179. Schiller called Wolf's account 'barbaric'. See James I. Porter, *Nietzsche and the Philology of the Future* (Stanford: Stanford University Press, 2000), p. 311. On Wolf's *Prolegomena* as 'the first modern history of an ancient text', see Anthony Grafton, *Commerce with the Classics: Ancient Books and Renaissance Readers* (Ann Arbor: The University of Michigan Press, 1997), p. 174.

9. Moore and Aveling's translation is felicitous in echoing the original author of the term and the concept 'bathos'

in English: Alexander Pope. Pope satirically argued that in the current 'flourishing' state of British trade (in 1728), language, like other natural materials used in manufacture, was subject to the 'Golden Rule of Transformation', namely, that any object or value can be turned into its opposite and diminished to the point of absurdity in the interests of trade. Bathos is the good practice of this Golden Rule, the 'the *non plus ultra* of true Modern Poesie!' (*Peri Bathous: The Art of Sinking in Poetry*, in *Prose Works of Alexander Pope: Volume 2*, p. 186). On bathos, see Chapter 3 of this volume.

10. Louis Althusser, 'Preface to *Capital: Volume One*' (1969), in *Lenin and Philosophy and Other Essays* (Ben Brewster trans.) (London: New Left Books, 1971), p. 92.

11. Ibid., pp. 71, 74.

12. Karl Kautsky, *The Economic Doctrines of Karl Marx* (H. J. Stenning trans.) (London: A. & C. Black, 1925), p. 11.

13. Samuel Beckett, *Molloy; Malone Dies; The Unnamable* (London: Calder, 1997), p. 139.

14. Kautsky, *Economic Doctrines*, p. 11.

15. J. Hillis Miller, 'Promises, Promises: Speech Act Theory, Literary Theory, and Politico-Economic Theory in Marx and de Man', *New Literary History* 33(1) (Winter 2002): 1–20. Quoted from p. 7.

16. Guy Debord's most direct commentary on *détournement* is an article co-authored with Gil Wolman, 'Mode d'emploi du détournement' (1956), in Guy Debord, *Œuvres* (Jean-Louis Rançon and Alice Debord eds) (Paris: Gallimard, 2006). For a practical guide to *détournement* that

gives examples of the method in action, see Debord's 'Relevé provisoire des citations et des détournements de *La Société du spectacle*', in ibid. Debord wrote this 'provisional statement' in 1973 for the translators of his famous text, to make sure that they would preserve intact its artifice of parodic and transformed literary citations (many of which are transformed citations of *Le Capital*).

17. Theodor W. Adorno, 'Thesen über Bedürfnis' (1942), in *Gesammelte Schriften* (Rolf Tiedemann ed.), VOL. 8 (Frankfurt am Main: Suhrkamp, 1972), p. 392 (my translation).

18. Marx, *Capital*, VOL. 2, p. 223.

19. The first definition of 'congeal' in *A Copious and Critical English–Latin Lexicon founded on the German-Latin Dictionary of Dr. Charles Ernest Georges* (Londinii: Longman, Brown, Green, and Longmans, 1847) is 'to freeze', then 'to cause or make to *c, congelare* (by letting athg get cold)'.

20. For a recent account of living labour as 'the fundamental human faculty' trapped in agonistic opposition with abstract labour, see Michael Hardt and Antonio Negri, *Multitude: War and Democracy in the Age of Empire* (London: Penguin, 2006), pp. 144–6.

21. *Meyers Konversations-Lexicon*, VOL. 6 (Leipzig: 1888), p. 857 (my translation). The German text is accessible online at http://peter-hug.ch/lexikon/1888_bild/06_0857

22. For the most famous and seminal passage on the division of labour, which takes as its example the 'very trifling manufacture' of pins, see Adam Smith, *An Inquiry into the Nature and Causes of the Wealth of Nations* (R. H. Campbell and A. S. Skinner eds) (Oxford: Clarendon, 1979), pp. 14–15.

23. Cf. Karl Marx and Friedrich Engels, *The German Ideology*
(C. J. Arthur ed.) (London: Lawrence & Wishart, 1974),
p. 103: 'Philosophy and the study of the actual world have
the same relation to one another as masturbation and
sexual love.' A satirical remark at the expense of puritanical readers disgusted by the obscene, no doubt; but also
a suggestion that the appetite for the study of phantoms
and the satisfaction to be gained from it is, at a basic level,
identical to the appetite for and satisfaction to be gained
from the study of material. For Althusser, Marx stopped
masturbating once and for all when he discovered sexual
love in the bower of scientific bliss; but might not a little
permanent recidivism in this case be the spice of new life?

24. Ibid., p. 47.

25. William Cowper, *The Task*, BK 2, lines 563–4, in *The
Poems of William Cowper: Volume 2, 1782-1785* (John D.
Baird and Charles Ryskamp eds) (Oxford: Clarendon,
1995), p. 153. Marx sees in what the bourgeoisie finds
bathetic the image of bourgeois culture itself. The bourgeoisie itself creates the stage and the mirror and all the
instruments of vanity that it loathes. It engenders and
then acts the censor and diagnostician of its own bathos.
For Cowper as for Pope, bathos is the name of an offence
against natural truth and value; for Marx, bourgeois
bathos is the literary symptomatology of bourgeois economic success.

26. Cf. Marx and Engels:

> Since in the fully formed proletariat the abstraction
> of all humanity, even of the semblance of humanity,
> is practically complete; since the conditions of life

of the proletariat sum up all the conditions of life of society today in their most inhuman form; since man has lost himself in the proletariat, yet at the same time has not only gained theoretical consciousness of that loss, but through urgent no longer removable, no longer disguisable, absolutely imperative *need*—the practical expression of *necessity*—is driven directly to revolt against this inhumanity, it follows that the proletariat can and must emancipate itself (*The Holy Family*, pp. 36–7).

27. The phrase is by Ernst Bloch, cited in Georg Lukács, 'Realism in the Balance' in *Aesthetics and Politics* (London: New Left Books, 1977), p. 42.

28. Karl Marx, *The Eighteenth Brumaire of Louis Bonaparte: Later Political Writings* (Terrell Carver ed. and trans.) (Cambridge: Cambridge Univeristy Press, 1996), p. 120.

29. 'This person must [. . .] be swept out of the way, and made impossible' [Karl Marx and Friedrich Engels, *The Communist Manifesto* (Samuel Moore trans.) (London: Penguin, 2002), p. 238]

30. Charles de Brosses, *Du Culte des Dieux Fétiches, ou Parallèle de l'ancienne Religion de l'Egypte avec la Religion actuelle de Nigritie* (Westmead: Gregg International, 1972 [1760]), p. 237.

31. Chateaubriand, *Itinéraire de Paris a Jérusalem* (Paris: Garnier-Flammarion, 1968 [1811]), p. 373 (my translation).

32. The origin of the now 'Marxist' word and concept 'fetishism' in De Brosses was pointed out by, inter alia, Mikhail Lifshitz, *The Philosophy of Art of Karl Marx*

(Ralph B. Winn trans.) (London: Pluto Press, 1973), p. 36. On the contribution of De Brosses's commentary to the history of the concept in general, see Roy Ellen, 'Fetishism', *Man: New Series* 23(2) (1988): 213–35.

33. 'Segui il tuo corso, e lascia dir le genti', instead of 'Vien retro a me, e lascia dir le genti' [Dante, *Purgatorio*, canto 5, line 13]. Incidentally, Régis Debray mistakes Marx's *détournement* of Dante for the sweet new style of the original: '"*Segui il tuo corso e lascia dir le genti*"—conseil de Dante au chercheur' [*La puissance et les rêves* (Paris: Gallimard, 1984), p. 117]

34. Althusser, *Lenin and Philosophy*, p. 92.

35. V. I. Lenin, *Collected Works*, VOL. 38 (Moscow, 1963), p. 180.

36. Laura Mulvey, 'Some Thoughts on Theories of Fetishism in the Context of Contemporary Culture', *October* 65 (Summer 1993): 3–20. Quoted from p. 8.

37. Mulvey's account seems to follow Fredric Jameson, confirming without hesitation what he described as one possible option for interpreting Marx: '[I]f commodity fetishism can in one way be usefully described as "the effacement of the traces of production from the object", then aesthetic dereification will naturally enough be identified as the will to deconceal those traces' [*Signatures of the Visible* (London: Routledge, 1992), p. 188].

38. Mulvey, 'Some Thoughts on Theories of Fetishism': 9.

39. For the first appearance of the word and De Brosses's first defence of it, see *Du Culte des Dieux Fétiches*, p. 10.

40. Giorgio Agamben, *Stanzas: Word and Phantasm in West-*

ern Culture (Ronald L. Martinez trans.) (Minneapolis: University of Minnesota Press, 1993), p. 35.

41. De Brosses, *Du Culte des Dieux Fétiches*, p. 164. (All translations from De Brosses are my own.)

42. On what is today the obvious racism and mythographic licence of De Brosses's ethnography, see Peter Mark, 'Fetishers, "Marybuckes" and the Christian Norm: European Images of Senegambians and their Religions, 1550–1760', *African Studies Review* 23(2) (1980): 91–9. On De Brosses's parallel account of primitive language acquisition and the 'natural order', see Gérard Genette, *Mimologics* (Thaïs E. Morgan trans.) (Lincoln: University of Nebraska Press, 1994), pp. 65–90.

43. Heidegger's neo-Schillerian discourse on the status of objects for primitives is in *Being and Time*:

> [F]or primitive man, the sign coincides with that which is indicated. Not only can the sign represent this in the sense of serving as a substitute for what it indicates, but it can do so in such a way that the sign itself always *is* what it indicates. This remarkable coinciding does not mean, however, that the sign-Thing has already undergone a certain 'Objectification'—that it has been experienced as a mere Thing and misplaced into the same realm of Being of the present-at-hand as what it indicates. This 'coinciding' is not an identification of things which have hitherto been isolated from each other: it consists rather in the fact that the sign has not as yet become free from that of which it is a sign.

Such a use of signs is still absorbed completely in Being-towards what is indicated, so that a sign as such cannot detach itself at all [Martin Heidegger, *Being and Time* (John Macquarrie and Edward Robinson trans.) (New York: Harper Collins, 1962), p. 113].

44. De Brosses, *Du Culte des Dieux Fétiches*, p. 201. Nietzsche, of course, raised this conventional gesture of astonishment and its emphasis on the mutuality of the enlightened to an art and a philosophy in itself. A dividend of the same impulse is still at work in the majority of Lacan's writing, though often in bafflingly crude form: 'Do not, however, get the idea that I address myself to everyone at large. I am speaking to those who are savvy, to the nonidiots' [Jacques Lacan, *Television: A Challenge to the Psychoanalytic Establishment* (Joan Copjec ed., Denis Hollier, Rosalind Kraus and Annette Michelson trans.) (New York: Norton, 1990), p. 3].

45. De Brosses, *Du Culte des Dieux Fétiches*, p. 12.

46. Ibid., pp. 184–6.

47. Cf. Benjamin Constant: 'L'étonnement de la première jeunesse, à l'aspect d'une société si factice et si travaillée, annonce plutôt un cœur naturel qu'un esprit méchant' [*Adolphe* (Paris: Flammarion, 1989), pp. 54–5]; 'The astonishment of early youth at the sight of so artificial and so complicated a society reveals a natural heart rather than an evil disposition' [*Adolphe* (Margaret Mauldon trans.) (Oxford: Oxford University Press, 2001), p. 11].

48. 'Enlightenment is mankind's exit from its self-incurred immaturity [*selbstverschuldeten Unmündigkeit*]' [Immanuel

Kant, 'An Answer to the Question: What Is Enlightenment?' in *What Is Enlightenment? Eighteenth-Century Answers and Twentieth-Century Questions* (James Schmidt ed.) (Berkeley: University of California Press, 1996), 58]. The maturity of the enlightened individual in Kant's sense is a kind of autonomy and self-determination. Marx's description of the commodity in Part 1, Section 3 of *Capital* is a satirical negative mirror image of the enlightened *mündig* person, as well as a contribution to the larger theoretical account of his present impossibility: 'Since no commodity can stand in the relation of equivalent to itself, and thus turn its own bodily shape into the expression of its own value, every commodity is compelled to choose some other commodity for its equivalent, and to accept the use-value, that is to say, the bodily shape of that other commodity as the form of its own value' [MA: 65]. Marx is using the commodity as a marionette to satirize the *unmündig* person, whose realist theoretical portrait is given in Adorno's description of compulsory psychic compromise enforced by capitalism: '[the] individual must harmoniously stylize the contrary course of the world and heteronomously obey it, against his own better insight' [Theodor W. Adorno, *Negative Dialectics* (E. B. Ashton trans.) (London: Routledge, 1973), p. 152].

49. M. V. David, 'Les idées du 18e siècle sur l'idolâtrie, et les audaces de David Hume et du Président de Brosses', *Numen* 24(2) (1977): 81–94. Quote from p. 91 (my translation).

50. A passing comment on Marx's interest in De Brosses is made by Jean-Luc Nancy, 'The Two Secrets of the Fetish'

(Thomas C. Platt trans.), *Diacritics* 31(2) (Summer, 2001): 2–8: Quote from p. 4. Terrell Carver twice notes the derivation but makes no comment on it except to say, inaccurately, that 'Marx used the word "fetish" in this [i.e. De Brosses's] eighteenth- and nineteenth-century sense' ['Marx's Commodity Fetishism', *Inquiry* 18 (1975): 39–63. Quote from p. 50]. Cf. Terrell Carver, *The Postmodern Marx* (Manchester: Manchester University Press, 1998), p. 15, where he suggests that we bring interpretations of Marx up to date by subjecting his works to the full pressure and illumination of postmodern hermeneutics (but this means, for Carver, deference to already existing poststructuralist theories of interpretation like Foucault's 'regime of truth', etc.). Marx is not treated as literature that requires close reading but as text that requires a theory of textuality. Cf. Ernesto Laclau's review of *The Postmodern Marx*, where the consequences of this treatment are manifested in the admiring jargon of theoretical recuperation:

> A great deal of literature has tried to discover the 'true' Marx, but we get from Carver a fascinating unveiling of the multiplicity of the Marxian text, of the various discursive sequences whose unity results from contingent articulations rather than from any underlying univocal principle. Seen from this angle, the work of Marx appears as a sort of microcosm in which we find, in nuce, all the potential and often contradictory trends of the history of Marxism in the century following the founder's death [Ernesto Laclau, review of *The*

Postmodern Marx, by Terrell Carver, *American Political Science Review* 95(4) (2001): 976].

51. Slavoj Žižek, *The Plague of Fantasies* (London: Verso, 1997), p. 98.

52. Žižek never cites the De Brosses directly, but says in a footnote that he draws on the work of Alfonzo Iacono (ibid., p. 124).

53. Ibid., p. 105.

54. Marshall Berman writes, '[T]he audience [of *Capital*] finds itself onstage' [*Adventures in Marxism* (London: Verso, 1999), p. 85]. I would add: *and nowhere else.*

55. As the entry on 'commodity fetishism' by Ben Fine in Tom Bottomore's 'Up-to-date Guide to the Basic Concepts of Marxism' [*A Dictionary of Marxist Thought*, 2nd edn (Oxford: Blackwell, 1991), p. xii] puts it, '[t]he simplicity of commodity fetishism makes it a starting point and example for analysing non-economic relations. It establishes a dichotomy between appearance and concealed reality (without the former necessarily being false) which can be taken up in the analysis of IDEOLOGY' (ibid., p. 102). There is no mention of De Brosses either in this entry or in the entry on 'fetishism' by Michèle Barrett, in ibid., p. 190.

56. Nancy, 'Two Secrets of the Fetish', p. 6.

57. An excellent philological account of this tradition of commentary is Pierre Hadot, *The Veil of Isis: An Essay on the History of the Idea of Nature* (Michael Chase trans.) (Cambridge, MA.: Harvard University Press, 2006).

58. Žižek, *Plague of Fantasies*, p. 105.

59. Theodor W. Adorno, *The Jargon of Authenticity* (Knut Tarnowski and Frederic Will trans.) (London: Routledge, 2003), p. 43.

Wrong Poetry

try to whistle / with a tooth broken

PROLOGUE: LITERALIZATION

i

In the great 'Preface' to his *Phenomenology of Spirit*, Hegel makes a cutting observation about knowledge. Faced with the sorts of radical demands on thinking made by his own speculative philosophy, knowledge (*Wissen*) tends, in the first instance, to react defensively. It acts up, squirms, revels in phlegmatics, grabs for what it already owns or contains, eulogizes over its abstractions, asserts the unarguableness and even the divinity of its intuitions; above all, it 'recount[s] conventional ideas as if they were established and familiar truths'.[1] Hegel's 'Science' cannot be studied unless the candidate 'knowledge' be ready to leave off making a spectacle of itself like this, take a deep inspiring breath and 'take on' the 'strenuous effort of the concept'.[2] But knowledge, in Hegel's experience, is 'usually' not ready to do that. It usually is not, because it is invariably predisposed to identify a thought as 'true' by finding it to be familiar. As we know from our familiarity with dictums, to 'what oft was thought' belongs the best chance of being well expressed, and 'knowledge', Hegel observes, is usually in the first instance more preoccupied with 'recounting' its contents in irresistible style than it is interested in making any sort of strenuous effort (it was an important condition of Beckett's prose that this distinction should be impossible to believe in). The familiarity of 'truths'—'bekannte Wahrheiten', truths in the plural, as one might say 'the Bauers and Stirners' to dismiss them from singularity—is profoundly reassuring to this 'knowledge' whose reason for acting is in order to be reassured. It is reassuring not simply because it presents knowledge with a reason not to do anything new, so that knowledge may remain snug and warm (not in a dead end, but within its means, its 'living'), but also because it seems to establish that the purpose of experience has been, and may as well continue to be, to confirm that we are already having experiences in the right way. However bad our experiences may be, and they may sometimes even be moderately bad, we at least know very well how to have them. So at least our familiar truths would seem to attest; since if we did not already know very well how to have experiences, how could we ever have become familiar with truths? If we were really living a wrong life, let alone one that cannot be lived rightly, we surely could not have got on to such easygoing terms with truth; why then should we venture to abjure our familiarity with truths, for what on the face of it must seem the very perverse reason that we want to make life wrong after all? If we know very well how to have experiences, can a 'strenuous effort' to conceive everything otherwise than as it familiarly is, and as it might familiarly stay, be anything but an extravagance promising disorder, madness, infantilism or idiocy? And in any case, isn't the demand that we make a 'strenuous effort' unintelligible, not to say offensive, unless we can first be allowed to familiarize ourselves with the competition (who else gets to make this 'strenuous effort'?), calculate the outlay (just how strenuous, exactly?) and project our earnings (what do I get out of it?).

Knowledge always knows enough to know that it doesn't want to be cheated. No acquisition without due diligence.

Hegel's description of the primary reaction of knowledge to the sort of difficult and unfamiliar experience that 'speculative philosophy' must compulsorily involve is an incidental satire.[3] It is, on the face of it, a philosophical description of the behaviour of a mental faculty but it cannot be read except by thinking of living individuals whose cognitive credibility it demolishes. It is not a definition of

a concept, simply, such as we are too much in the habit of
thinking that we find in Kant, or even in Marx; it is also
a moment of disguised social commentary in which the
disguise is provocatively flimsy. Its most unmistakably
satirical conduct is precisely that it does not openly present itself as what it is, namely, an attack on philistines, but
that this attack is instead carried out under cover of a
superficial discursive equanimity, the discursive equanimity of 'philosophy' or 'Science', an equanimity sponsored
in part by the 'abstractions' (knowledge, truth, intuition,
freedom, etc.) whose behaviour this passage in the 'Preface' anatomizes. It is, on the face of it, a discussion of the
behaviour of that impersonal (because universal) thing—
'knowledge'—when it first encounters that not invidiously
specified but perfectly anonymous thing—'something unfamiliar'. Any resemblance to actual persons may indeed
not be accidental, since, after all, actual persons are where
knowledge tends to hang out; but, as we learn later in the
Phenomenology, Hegel is not pointing at anything that
can say 'I' and mean by that pronoun himself and only
himself.

> Of course, what has been said here [in the foregoing
> paragraphs of the 'Preface'] does express the concept,
> but cannot count for more than an anticipatory assur-
> ance. Its truth does not lie in this partly narrative
> exposition, and is therefore just as little refuted
> by asserting the contrary, by calling to mind and

recounting conventional ideas, as if they were established and familiar truths, or by dishing up something new with the assurance that it comes from the shrine of inner divine intuition. A reception of this kind is usually the first reaction on the part of knowing [Reaction des Wissens] to something unfamiliar [etwas unbekannt]; it resists it in order to save its own freedom and its own insight, its own authority, from the alien authority (for this is the guise in which what is newly encountered first appears), and to get rid of the appearance that something has been learned and of the sort of shame this is supposed to involve.[4]

One recent commentator on the 'Preface' gets around the awkwardly too abstract and German idea that an abstraction like 'knowledge' might too humanly 'react', 'resist' and try to 'save its own freedom' by making a new English translation which argues that Hegel was not using 'knowledge' as an abstract concept that seems unavoidably also to refer to living individuals but that he was directly naming living individuals with an abstract noun. In Yirmiyahu Yovel's version, published in 2005, the long and complex last sentence in the passage quoted above is done like this (the additions in square brackets are Yovel's own):

Such is the usual [negative] reception which [the world of] knowledge reserves to what is unfamiliar—it reacts with resistance to it, in order to save its own freedom, its own insight and authority, from the

> authority of a foreigner (since those we meet for the
> first time are perceived as foreigners); and also in order
> to remove the appearance of a certain kind of shame
> which supposedly lies in learning something.[5]

Yovel's Hegel is not only making a number of points different from anything in Miller's but he is making them
with a different sort of reader in mind. Did Hegel simply
neglect to specify that the reaction of knowledge to the
unfamiliar thing is 'negative', so that Yovel is justified in
completing that thought for him, or did Hegel have a
reason not to use that important predicate in his description of what 'knowledge' does? What, or who, did Hegel
mean by 'knowledge'? Is the 'Reaction des Wissens' an
innuendo, or could it just be abstract German shorthand,
not intended to insinuate anything about anyone but used
to explicitly identify a social group? Whereas Miller's
Hegel resists actually pointing his finger, and so leaves it
to the imagination of his reader to pick out the phantom
trajectory of its allegation, Yovel's Hegel is candid, upright,
perhaps a little lofty, certainly a little Horatian. He is not
the scourge of reactionary behaviour but its therapist or
corrector. He has patience enough for the likely confusion
of a reader confronted with ambiguity to explain his
abstractions by literalizing them into familiar social types.
It may be that nothing but living individuals can be meant
by Hegel's 'knowledge', but Yovel's Hegel cushions his

reader against the uncomfortable suspicion that she may herself be the direct object of his German ancestor's anatomical observation by refining the abstraction into an Augustan generality: not *you and your knowledge*, dear reader of this book, but 'the world of knowledge' is reactionary in the face of what is unfamiliar. The equanimity in that expression is not superficial but thorough; it is the equanimity of a responsible Johnsonian surveyor of human folly. Its conventional diagnosis may be familiarly agreed with; in fact, the best way to agree with its diagnosis is familiarly, since by allowing the justice of the observation (that 'the world of knowledge' tends to react badly to unfamiliar things) on familiar terms we reciprocate the generosity shown by Yovel's Hegel in his care to explain to us the abstraction 'knowledge' by therapeutically literalizing it.[6]

Yovel's Hegel thinks that when we meet them for the first time we perceive people as foreigners. That is either a very obviously untrue suggestion or a curiously pathological one, depending on whether we want Hegel to be stupid or ill; unless it is a profound remark that insinuates a theological generality about our being sunk into universal alienation, the sort of thought that must owe its bottom to what Hegel in this same passage mockingly calls 'the shrine of inner divine intuition'. (In any case, it as if accidentally makes Hegel's thought into the direct contradiction of Wordsworth's hope that we might live in a place 'where if we meet a face / We almost meet a friend'.)[7] Those we meet for the first time, Yovel's Hegel explains, we perceive as foreigners, and the authority of foreigners threatens the freedom of the world of knowledge. The world of knowledge is for Yovel's Hegel in that case the proud owner of an extraordinarily vulnerable freedom, since everyone not already known to it stands in relation to its freedom as a potential destroyer, at least insofar as he has any authority. The best course of defensive action for the world of knowledge must in this case be either to meet no one or to meet only those people who can be counted on to have no authority, like the children or employees of its members.

I make this loud Juvenalian reply to Yovel's in truth just faintly Horatian adaptation of Hegel for two reasons, besides the significantly irresistible pleasure of writing satire derivative from Marx's satire.

First, it is an answer to Yovel's remark in the 'Preface' to his translation that he has 'followed the letter of the original Hegelian text [. . .] using straightforward contemporary style and avoiding literary embellishment'. Yovel describes how he did this: 'I broke Hegel's long sentences, or simplified their structure. I also omitted his italics.'[8] Every reader of Beckett will know that literature is not so easily avoided, and that nothing embellishes like simplification and omission. As for 'straightforward contemporary style', Yovel has a great many contemporaries, and many of them have styles, and many of those styles repudiate each other aggressively; some of them are even straightforward in ways that would probably strike Yovel as unintelligibly devious. There are, of course, more or less objectively more or less straightforward ways of putting things, but that is itself a very complex fact whose exposition usually depends on the implicit nomination of deviants (in this case, 'literary' translators, the abstainers from omission).

Second, I think that Yovel's translation of this passage substitutes a plainly intelligible but very probably untrue thought belonging to Yovel's Hegel for a difficult thought whose truth exists only insofar as it remains to be established by the strenuous effort actually to experience contradiction of it. If Hegel is right that 'knowledge' must grow out of the behaviour he describes (and it is worth noting that this growth of the philosopher's mind would not be the ideally direct or continuous progress from 'immaturity' to 'maturity' commended by Kant in his essay on the meaning of 'enlightenment'), it will not succeed simply by subordinating its ambiguity to its explanation.[9] Instead, as we will see, knowledge must experience contradiction to the point of losing itself. Yovel literalizes the abstraction in Hegel, making 'knowledge' into 'the world of knowledge', the familiar Augustan figure for a community of learned individuals. ('[T]he propriety of each of these lines has been celebrated by writers whose opinion the world has reason to regard', Samuel Johnson commented on some passages from Milton. 'I shall here endeavour (for the Benefit of my Countrymen) to make it manifest, that Epick Poems may be made *without a Genius*, nay without Learning or much Reading. This must necessarily be of great Use to all those Poets who confess they never Read, and of whom the World is convinced they never Learn,' wrote Pope in earnest, offering his therapy of instruction.)[10] Yovel's is a bad literalization, both for being too decisive and for being exclusively motivated by the wish to explain. Yovel's literalization is bad not simply in that it misidentifies the individuals whose behaviour Hegel mockingly anatomized with the use of his apparently just philosophical concept 'knowledge' (Hegel did not, I think, mean for us to understand that it is the community of intellectuals who behave in the way he describes knowledge behaving) but also because it deletes the satire in this passage of the 'Preface' by adopting an attitude of genuine equanimity in place of Hegel's impossibly superficial imitation of equanimity. 'In order to write easily,' Pope decided in the context of an essay on pastoral, 'it is necessary, in the first place, to think easily.'[11] The straightforward style free of embellishment has for

centuries been metonymic for a testimony of good con-
science, the expression of spirit untroubled by moral or
material adversity. In the passage from Miller's Hegel, the
abstraction 'knowledge' stays abstract (Adorno will later
insist that, for negative dialectics, what is negated stays
negated); but it is just that difficult, irreducible difference
from direct sociological pointing and identifying, the difference from *naming names*, that opens up by satirical
deviation the space for a much more intensely implied
anatomy of the philistine fussing over his alibi for cognitive inertia. It is by being strenuously insisted upon that
abstraction comes nearest to life, not by being evacuated
in order that an already familiar identity from life can be
granted a local habitation in it by way of sinecure. In other
words, abstraction is not always a placeholder for a personal or material identity, a cipher that elicits an explanatory human content. It may just as well be a renunciation
of explanations of the type whose invariable recourse is to
sociological pointing and identifying; it may even be a
satire against that type of explanation, and devious enough
to renounce sociological identification only in order to
point with hyperbolic narrowness at a single individual,
the person defined by 'knowledge' whose unmentionable
name is 'you'.

The increasing complexity of these remarks on a
single passage from Hegel's 'Preface' may suggest that the

effort to read the passage is beginning to get strenuous, as Hegel thought it ought to. To test that possibility, it may be worth setting out, and pressing forward, some of the thinking so far in the form of questions. When we call 'knowledge' in this passage from the 'Preface' an abstraction, what sort of abstraction do we have in mind? Is it an abstraction that elicits a particular human content to complete its meaning: an individual, for example, or a familiar group like '[the world of] knowledge'; or is it an abstraction that renounces any particular content designed to complete it by explaining it, since an explanatory content must invariably be 'recounted' like a 'conventional idea'? Does it not only rely for its intelligibility on the idea or semblance that it elicits a particular human content? Does it also in a more direct and practical way solicit a particular content from that unnamable and anonymous person, whoever she is, the living individual who is right now, at this moment, the reader of the 'Preface'? Does Hegel mean for a reader who is *his* reader to literalize 'knowledge' into the figure of a person, which might possibly be the person with the name 'you'? If Hegel does mean for her to do that, is she also meant to understand it to be a test of her aptitude to be his reader, or her aptitude for what he tells her is 'speculative philosophy'? In other words, will she be a better speculative philosopher if, having recognized a description of living individuals in

Hegel's account of the behaviour of 'knowledge', she then decisively identifies those individuals with 'knowledge' and thereby confirms that the abstraction is a social satire? Or would she do better to hold back from making a decisive identification, so that the abstraction may be ambiguously satirical rather than positively satirical? Is the answer to all these questions that the reader will herself become the individual identifed as 'knowledge' the moment she decides that she has the answer to any of them, or even at the moment she decides that she has asked all the right questions? Is the confrontation of that unfamiliar risk, the risk of relegating myself into the object of the satire that I make a strenuous effort to identify, itself an instance of what Hegel describes as the confrontation with 'something unfamiliar'?

One thing it may mean to follow Marx in his well-known but perhaps inadequately and insufficiently examined claim that Hegel's speculative philosophy is 'ideological' to the extent that it mistakes real individuals in class society for abstractions like 'knowledge' is that the satirical dimension of passages like this one from the 'Preface' must be strenuously insisted upon. For (what with a satirically therapeutic omission of the usual anxiety over the difficulties of calling anyone 'Marxist' I will call) a Marxist reader of the 'Preface', Hegel's observation about the behaviour of knowledge *is really* an anatomical remark about real individuals. It is, for the historical materialist in truth, a satire at the expense of a specific social type. Speculative philosophy in Hegel's sense may not be intended as a positive sociology; but for a Marxist reader, the most pressing confrontation with the unfamiliar thing is defined not by the logical risk of relegating herself into the object of the satire whose presence she confirms but by the practical work of directing that satire against the most important social target. The Marxist reader may indeed be the object of Hegel's satire but she alone cannot be its most important individual target; and the social irrelevance of her self-identification as the object of satire will be the more glaring the more pathos seems to accrue to that private act, and the more important it is to identify and attack the real target. So what, on these terms, is the real target? Who is 'knowledge'?[12]

Before we answer that question, it is important to remember that for Marx, no less than for Hegel, social philosophy must be dialectical and speculative: not simply positive. The insistence that the text is a satire does not equal a wish to make it into a cipher that can simply be decoded like a clumsy allegory: by, for example, connecting the pigs to the dictators; we have to think the identity of the object of satire, not just look it up or call it 'the philistine' or 'the mass'. Plenty of individuals more or less continuously avoid the 'strenuous effort of the concept'.

There never lived anyone who never avoided it. Is Hegel's real target in this passage the behaviour of everyone who ever avoided the effort, that is, everyone on earth? Is the passage a theological stricture on universal insufficiency? It seems unlikely, because not everyone protests unreasonable demands by referring the unfamiliar thing to his 'shrine of inner divine intuition', like a farcical proto-Victorian Tiresias (or Tiresiana). Is it then a satire against people who defend their right to indolence with the use of conservative, self-flattering or religiose language? If it is, then its satire is of a sort already long familiar, one that was a special preoccupation of English poetry of the eighteenth century. It would be the digusted mockery of the slothful and supine, overfed and underexercised existence that no reader could fail to identify as belonging to the average male aristocrat, whatsoever might be the 'abstractions' and epithets shuffled up to make his portrait distractingly generic. Cowper, whose famous poem *The Task*, published in 1785, begins with a panegyric to the sofa, gave the standard sort of account:

> The sedentary stretch their lazy length
> When custom bids, but no refreshment find,
> For none they need: the languid eye, the cheek
> Deserted of its bloom, the flaccid, shrunk,
> And wither'd muscle, and the vapid soul,
> Reproach their owner with that love of rest

> To which he forfeits even the rest he loves.
> Not such th' alert and active.[13]

The sedentary do not make the strenuous effort of the concept. They act as 'Custom bids', witheringly reiterating conventional ideas as if they were established and familiar truths. Not such the alert and active historical materialist. Can we read Hegel like that? Not, I think, as Marxists, because 'the sedentary' in Cowper's satire are specifically literalized into the decadent upper end of the unproductive classes in Marx: they are the aristocracy; and for Marx it was no longer the aristocracy who made the most significantly vapid conventional appeal to 'the shrine of inner divine intuition', or whose interests were defended by 'established and familiar truths'. Under capitalism, carrying on like that had become the prerogative of the bourgeoisie.

A Marxist reading of the 'Preface' to *Phenomenology of Spirit* is one that strenuously literalizes the abstraction 'knowledge' into the social type 'bourgeois consciousness'. But what sort of literalization is that? Literalization in Marx's own writing is rarely, if ever, just a matter of making explicit the content of a thought, or of referring a metaphor to a material object or state of affairs, or an idea to a person, or (as Marx himself sometimes epigrammatically imagined his response to Hegel's philosophy) of restoring the proper order of subject and predicate in 'speculative propositions' by turning Hegel on his head.[14]

When he belabours the 'German' philosopher addled on abstractions with 'the *real man*', his cudgel of human italics; or when he explains that for any man who is not the abstraction 'Man', the sublime region called in the language of philosophy 'the main seat of sensuality' is his penis; or to take a more pressing example, when he defines wage labour as the 'productive expenditure of human brains, nerves, and muscles', Marx is not just literalizing a phantom into an anatomy, or keeping thought free from the 'fear' of phantomaticity that Derrida thinks Marx must avoid because it 'is not good for the serenity of research and the analytic distinction of concepts'.[15] Nor is he adopting Lenin's 'deliberately naïve belief of mankind' in order to establish (as Lenin argued that that belief must be used to establish) a foundation for a 'theory of knowledge'.[16] Literalization in Marx is generic transformation: it invariably means the introduction of satire. Or to reverse the order of subject and predicate in that proposition: Marx introduces satire by literalizing. He introduces it because it is there; the optic of Marx's historical materialism is bent on the disclosure of satire, and that bent is its conscious truth. There may be a sense in which it is wrong to say that the main seat of sensuality in a *real man* is his penis, and yet whatever truth may be attached to that denial will seem negligible in the optic of Marx's historical materialism, because the denial does not disclose satire but eliminates it (likewise, it may be wrong to say that sexuality is the deep motive pressure behind kindness; but there is not much truth to that denial in the optic of Freudian psychoanalysis because it is a denial that functions to confine the operation of sexuality rather than to universalize it). What counts as 'bad literalization' in Yovel's version of the 'Preface' is the promotion of Hegel's abstraction 'knowledge' into sociological disambiguity, according to the decision that by 'knowledge' Hegel meant the world of knowledge, incidentally an Augustan metonym for the society of intellectuals; bad literalization in Marx is whatever sort of focus on facts and objects functions to deaden contradiction by eliminating satire.

A Marxist reading will not simply point out that the description of the behaviour of knowledge in the 'Preface' is satirical. Dialectical identification of the necessity of satire means understanding that the satire must be there, but that it is there, and can only be there, only for the reader whose confrontation with the object of satire is a conscious, practical confrontation with its real social target. This idea of the reader is itself a speculative construction. It is the speculative construction of a reader who appreciates that truth must have, and can only have, a confrontational form. Satire is a confrontational form of truth. It is irreducibly social. For that reason, satire is, in Marx's thinking, implicitly a form of literalization.

Whatever Marx himself may have written to the contrary, Marx's historical materialism does not begin when speculative philosophy ends. It begins when the art of expressing truth in its most confrontational form makes speculative philosophy into a practice of strenuous literalization.

A Marxist editor of Miller's Hegel might present the passage from the 'Preface' like this (the Marxist proliferation of italics is a sort of comical iconography of 'strenuous effort' at explanation—Marxist italicization is invariably *détournement*; the Marxist interpolations in square brackets are from the Althusserian perspective a grubby infringement on the pure theoretical meaning of the passage, just as Marx himself would have wished):

> Its truth does not lie in this partly narrative exposition, and is therefore just as little refuted by asserting the contrary, by *calling to mind* and *recounting conventional ideas*, as if they were *established and familiar truths*, or by *dishing up something new* with the assurance that it comes from the *shrine of inner divine intuition*. A *reception* of this kind is usually the first reaction on the part of *knowing* to something unfamiliar [and by *knowing* is meant the German bourgeois philosopher, arrogantly abstracting himself to a faculty]; it resists it in order to save its own *freedom* [which is the freedom for the stupid to starve] and its own *insight* [which comes fresh from the *shrine of*

inner divine intuition], its own *authority* [*possessed* as a
privilege from heaven!], from the *alien authority* [which
is the authority of the alien, who is nonetheless a slave
to our philosopher's benevolence in the dispensation
of wages] (for this [gentle readers] is the guise in
which what is newly encountered first appears), and
to *get rid of the appearance that something has been
learned* [since that something must turn out to be his
own inhumanity] and of the sort of *shame* this is supposed to involve [according to the lascivious homilies
of this evening's hostess].

ii

Confronted with the unfamiliar thing, knowledge at first
tries to reject what it learns. It tries to do that by fending
off the unfamiliar thing. Like Marx's bourgeois, knowledge reacts bristlingly to impingements on its freedom by
'Spirit'; like the bourgeois, it thinks its authority is endan-
gered by the coming authority of '*die fremde*', the alien and
barbaric; and like the bourgeois, it is in fact right to feel
threatened.[17] Because bourgeois consciousness is right to
feel threatened by the unfamiliar thing, its defensive
theatricalism is right for it too: the aggressive resort to
conventional ideas and established truths is, in a satirical
phrase that Marx used to attack the real target Jeremy
Bentham, 'genius in the way of bourgeois stupidity'.[18]
In order that progress can be made on Hegel's 'way of

despair', a process of development that his Marxist reader must satirically literalize into 'history', all knowledge that works to petrify the science of Spirit by enduring just as it is right now, dead to shame, remaining free by enforcing paralysis, must be made to give way under the force of the negative.[19] The 'way of despair', or 'history', must be lined with its remains; dead knowledge is the lining of history, a makeweight for the brains of the living.

Adorno works out the literalization of 'knowledge' as satire in Section 44 of *Minima Moralia*:

> Nothing is more unfitting for an intellectual resolved on practising what was earlier called philosophy, than to wish, in discussion, and one might almost say in argumentation, to be right. The very wish to be right [*das Rechtbehaltenwollen*], down to its subtlest form of logical reflection, is an expression of that spirit of self-preservation [*Selbsterhaltung*] which philosophy is precisely concerned to break down.[20]

'Knowledge' is the defensive bourgeois intellectual who engages in an argument only in order to win it, and who confronts the unfamiliar object only so that he may assert mastery over it. As Walter Benjamin wrote in one of his earliest essays, 'the philistine, you will have noted, only rejoices in every new meaninglessness. He remains in the right.'[21] The natural exercise of bourgeois consciousness is an exercise in being right. *Selbsterhaltung* and *das Rechtbehaltenwollen* mingle in one dead end of philistine compulsion. In the twilight of that false end, the 'newly encountered' unfamiliar thing takes on a specific objective aspect: it is a reagent; its menacingly catalytic substance is not to be grasped but to be dropped on impulse. It is an important consequence for Adorno's own Hegelian account of reading and of artworks that the bourgeois intellectual who remains in the right must thereby be disqualified from practising immanent criticism, because the object of immanent criticism, namely 'the substance grasped through the completed experience' of the work of art, is simply too expensive and onerous to get at (a Freudian might say the expense of spirit demanded by immanent criticism threatens castration of the bourgeois phallus).[22]

For Hegel, progress towards the goal of knowledge, that is, 'the point where knowledge no longer needs to go beyond itself, where knowledge finds itself', must forever involve 'conscious insight into the untruth' of knowledge.[23] Knowledge that acts to preserve itself by insisting that it is right must progressively learn not to *reject* wrong, since the attitude and practice of rejection are already familiar to it, but, more onerously, because more strenuously, to *become* wrong: becoming wrong is for knowledge the fundamental advance toward loss of itself. Knowledge must learn to be wrong to the point of perdition. As Hegel says, 'what is in fact the realization of the concept, counts for it [that is, for consciousness that takes itself to be knowledge] rather as the loss of its own self.'[24] This loss cannot be temporary or provisional, a mere blackout or reprimand; knowledge must irreversibly 'spoil its own limited satisfaction' by confrontation with the immanent unfolding of the unfamiliar thing, at the real and not imaginary or fantastical cost of its own freedom and authority.[25]

I want in this chapter to think carefully about the power of the unfamiliar thing to make knowledge, or the bourgeois intellectual, 'wish to be right', and the power of the unfamiliar thing to make knowledge, or the bourgeois intellectual, become wrong. Does the unfamiliar thing, Hegel's satirically anonymous *etwas unbekannt*, have any sort of essential aspect, substance or meaning? How does the unfamiliar thing appear to us, when we first acknowledge it, and later? What is our experience of an object long ago argued to belong to the category of unfamiliar things, or even established there, which we now confront for the first time, late in its history of provocation? What sort of object can qualify as an 'unfamiliar thing' whose power it is to make knowledge shrink into the overwrought postures of the philistine who remains in the right? Must the unfamiliarity of the object be reducible to conceptual unfamiliarity, or could it equally well be an irreducible unfamiliarity in sound, or in appearance? Can language be unfamiliar in Hegel's sense? Can poetry?

For Adorno, one very important unfamiliar object is the difficult artwork. The artwork that is radically difficult to understand ('incomprehensible' artworks do not belong to that category, as we shall see in a moment) often works as a taunt that stirs the philistine to a lot of familiar defensive ruses, the most typological and characteristic of which, Adorno thought, is the theatrical confession of modesty and incomprehension. Difficult artworks baffle, intimidate, stretch and upset. They do this not to only abuse the philistine, who may be the object and target of their satire, but, Adorno thinks, also to disabuse him. They do this by, first of all, identifying him. They tell him who he is. ('As a final truth, however: if you want to know who we are, just read Wordsworth's *Prelude*,' J. H. Prynne wrote to Ed Dorn on 6 November 1964.) The radically difficult artwork that identifies the philistine then unfolds to new extremes of both abuse and disabuse by provoking him into a 'negative relationship to truth', the first real step on Hegel's way of despair (which may be at a potentially misleading crossroads with the exit from the gallery into the cafe and gift shop). Difficult art does that by provoking philistine cognition into a *passionate* resistance against the object that endangers its own freedom and authority of judgement (we might say, a passionate attempt to recapture whatever escapes us, to get it securely pent up in what Emerson called our 'jail-yard of individual relations').[26]

Truth, wrote Wordsworth in the 'Preface' to *Lyrical Ballads*, must be 'carried alive into the heart by passion'. The 'negative relationship to truth' will be discovered, Marx wrote, in 'the hot passion [Leidenschaft] of truth' itself; elsewhere, Marx called criticism 'the head of passion'.[27] Readers of Lukács who regard him as programmatically or just inhumanly lacking in romanticism may be startled to read the following passage in his essay 'Marx and the Problem of Ideological Decay' (1938):

> The depth of the literary vision, of the realist approach to reality, is always passion [Leidenschaft]—no matter how the writer might formulate his world outlook intellectually—the passion not to accept anything as naked, cut and dried, dead experience, but to resolve the human world into a living inter-relationship between human beings. Whenever the prejudices of class society are too strong in a writer for him to do this, and he abandons this literary resolution of society into human relationships, then the writer ceases to be a realist.[28]

But for passion to be hot enough, and for passion to be strong enough to carry truth into the heart without killing it, or to reject dead experience, the artwork must itself be one whose unfolding will not trivialize passion or allow passion to become conventional and familiar. It must not 'recount' passion, in a gesture however sophisticatedly ironical, but demand it, live in it and bring life to it.

The difference between the practised, theatricalized rejection of an artwork, mere sarcastic head-scratching, and genuinely passionate resistance of its affront to our familiar powers of estimation or enjoyment, between witheringly just 'not getting it' on the one hand, and on the other *straining* to repudiate it as meaningless, idiotic, insulting or a violation of art, is, for Adorno, the difference between perorational stupefaction and the parturitive brilliancy of despair. The first response spectacularly goes nowhere: it is the dead end of bourgeois complacency and self-preservation; the second is a painful beginning, a trial run toward happiness.

The passionless dead end is described in an anatomical sketch full of ventriloquism in Section 139 of *Minima Moralia*:

> Cultivated philistines are in the habit of requiring that a work of art 'give' them something. They no longer take umbrage at works that are radical, but fall back on the shamelessly modest assertion that they do not understand. This eliminates even opposition, their last negative relationship to truth, and the offending object is smilingly catalogued among its kind, consumer commodities that can be chosen or refused without even having to take responsibility for doing so. One is just too stupid, too old-fashioned, one simply can't keep up, and the more one belittles oneself the more one can be sure of swelling the mighty unison of the

> *vox inhumana populi*, the judging power of the petri-
> fied Zeitgeist. Incomprehensibility, that benefits no-
> one, from being an inflammatory crime becomes
> pitiable folly.[29]

The experience of sheer incomprehension is no good for
anyone, left to conduct its own defence with its own philistine devices. Bourgeois consciousness invariably literalizes
the experience of getting no benefit from a difficult artwork by sociologically explaining it away as the natural
reaction to a very probably elitist attempt on its cognitive
virtue; the artwork that has the effrontery to make that
attempt cannot be allowed to be 'inflammatory', however
hot it may conceive its passion to be, since that would likely
identify it as satire, a concession that threatens to suggest
that its confrontation against the bourgeois may contain
some confrontational truth. Theatrical modesty is not just
a self-confirming sneer at the artwork but also a practical
contribution to its commodification. Notice that Adorno
does not say that the radical work *ought to be liked*, or that
its radical character should by itself necessarily command
any respect or admiration. *Minima Moralia* is not a panegyric to difficulty for its own sake, for example, of the sort
that Craig Raine defensively projects into the poetry of
Prynne, so that he, Craig Raine, can continue enjoying
without fuss or anxiety the emoluments of bourgeois
celebrity accruing to him in recognition of his established

truths about poetry. Adorno says instead that the familiar litany of rejoinders to difficult art ('one is just too stupid, too old-fashioned, one simply can't keep up . . . ') eliminates the 'last negative relationship to truth'. The familiar litany is a social masquerade but its consequence for the individual is to grind him to a real cognitive halt. Even sophisticatedly ironic self-preservation, *Selbsterhaltung* for the cleverly voluntarily outmoded, is nothing but a layby on the way of despair, a rest zone in which the passionate confrontation that leads knowledge to 'the loss of itself' can be traded in for what Hegel contemptuously calls 'shilly-shallying about this or that presumed truth': Frank O'Hara for Philip Larkin.[30] Hegel's exactingly unspecified object, *etwas unbekannt*, the unfamiliar thing, is here, in Adorno's scenario, 'smilingly catalogued among its kind', sale or return, itemized into the rolling product catalogue of humdrum novelties and hackneyed exotica. Just as Hegel's knowledge scrambles to 'get rid of the shame [*Schande*]' of learning something new, Adorno's philistines 'fall back on the shamelessly [*unverschämt*] modest assertion that they do not understand'.[31] What the philistine imagines is his smartly ironic confession of stupidity is in fact his real act of autostupefaction. Disingenuous avoidance of shame is the genuine foreclosure of insight.

My point in thinking about Hegel and Adorno together is not just to identify and comment on the reappearance of an Hegelian idea in *Minima Moralia*. More importantly for the present chapter, what the connection establishes is that Hegel's 'unfamiliar thing' is something that artists can make. Knowledge in the *Phenomenology* resists the unfamiliar thing much as the philistine in *Minima Moralia* resists radical art; but whereas Hegel's thing must be confronted because it is an unavoidable station on the way of despair, Adorno's radical art is confronted only if someone makes it, puts it out into the world, and argues for its significance. These may be descriptions of the same cognitive confrontation, but they are not descriptions of the same social confrontation. Adorno has literalized the argument from Hegel's 'Preface' into a satire on the murderously modest bourgeois father at the art gallery or poetry reading who is content to hear what the children like these days on condition that he may ban it from possession of any beauty or significance fit for adult consumption.

The social confrontation Adorno hopes for, a confrontation with the artwork that presses us into a truly and not just theatrically passionate reply, is by no means inevitable but contingent; in fact, in our present culture, which Adorno and Horkheimer ruthlessly satirized in *Dialectic of Enlightenment*, that confrontation is getting more improbable all the time. The culture industry is set up to delete it. Elsewhere in *Minima Moralia*, Adorno says that the social possibility of avoiding stupefaction is now so far from being freely or obviously available that the avoidance of stupefaction has become an 'almost insoluble task'.[32] For the task of despair to be soluble, for the cognitive halt of *Selbsterhaltung* and *das Rechtbehaltenwollen* to be prevented, there must be a practical and lived confrontation with genuinely radical art. That means, among a great many other contingencies, that someone has to make it. A moderately or predictably unfamiliar artwork will not do. As Prynne wrote in his still now violently unfamiliar sequence of poems *Down where changed* (1979), 'Nearly too much / is, well, nowhere near enough.'[33] The unfamiliar artwork cannot be *nearly* too odd or difficult, but ready all the more proudly to confirm us in our possession of established truths if we can just make that little bit of extra effort; it must be too much to bear without real loss. It cannot just stir up defensive reactions but must compel sublation of them. The artwork must produce and act as a sentinel over the 'negative relationship to truth', powerfully unfamiliar enough to compel 'real, active men' to renounce and transcend '*their* sort of happiness'.[34]

A question that comes into view at the end of this prologue to a confrontation with a radical artwork is whether we really need to accept that there is anything cognitively distinct about the experience of radical art. That question may not be conducive to a general answer that will be satisfying to everyone; it may be, like the radical artwork itself, a way of identifying whoever confronts it. But some consequences of an affirmative answer can be sketched out. If there is something cognitively distinct about the experience of radical art—if, that is, a poem can really have an immanent content that must and may only be attained through a strenuous effort, in Hegel's sense— then a sociology of the gestures, institutions and discourses of aesthetic radicalism or of the historical avant-gardes, however sophisticated, will not by itself be enough to explain radical art. An advanced sociological project like Bourdieu's *Distinction* (1984) would not, in that case, be any less enormously significant and useful for describing the social reality in which any social confrontation with a radical artwork must take place; but even the satirical sociology of *Distinction* must at last seem programmatically inarticulate about the power of radical art to transform the experience of knowledge. (To admit that limitation is not to champion Hegel *contra* sociology.)

What follows is a scholarly and critical confrontation with a single unfamiliar thing, a line of poetry that seemed to its first readers, and to many of its later readers too, difficult and radical. It is an effort to read the line *both* as a provocative move in what Bourdieu called 'the game of culture' *and* as art compelling cognitive transformation.[35] If I have a point to make about method, it is that immanent criticism of art and the sociology of art are not exclusive and irreconcilable options for thinking, however incompatible their results might seem and however much tension there might be between the exponents of either method, but that just that incompatibility and tension may, in fact, be the best evidence of their common necessity. More emphatically: the tension is the truth. A poem that seems wrong to the reader who wishes to be right and who is anxious to preserve his freedom and authority of judgement might be *both* a stride forward on the way of despair *and* a commodity whose invidious 'social function' is to 'legitimate social differences', both an advancement toward the goal of knowledge (whether or not that goal exists in social reality, or can really be reached) and 'objectively' a project for social self-advancement.[36] The *difficult* thing for a poet who knows this is not to make art that compels cognitive transformation but avoids being a plaything in the 'game of culture'; in a capitalist society, pure art like that is a fantasy just as profoundly bourgeois as theatricalized suspicion itself.[37] In fact, it is an idol of that suspicion. But neither can radical art just *smilingly catalogue* itself under the heading of this antinomy. The truly difficult thing for the poet is to make a poem that pronounces the antinomy in the most sociologically eloquent and cognitively strenuous form imaginable. No marketplace of playthings without the way of despair, and, more difficult yet, vice versa.

In his diary for 1815, Henry Crabb Robinson records the following conversation with William Wordsworth:

> *May 9th*. Took tea with the Lambs. Mr. and Mrs. Wordsworth were there. We had a long chat, of which, however, I can relate but little. Wordsworth, in answer to the common reproach that his sensibility is excited by objects which produce no effect on others, admits the fact, and is proud of it. He says that he cannot be accused of being insensible to the real concerns of life. He does not waste his feelings on unworthy objects, for he is alive to the actual interests of society. I think the justification is complete. If Wordsworth expected immediate popularity, he would betray an ignorance of public taste impossible in a man of observation. He spoke of the changes in his new poems. He has sub-stituted *ebullient* for *fiery*, speaking of the nightingale, and *jocund* for *laughing*, applied to the daffodils; but he will probably restore the original reading. But on my alluding to the lines,—
>
> 'Three feet long and two feet wide',
>
> and confessing that I dared not read them aloud in company, he said, 'They ought to be liked'.[38]

The line that Crabb Robinson found unspeakably embar-rassing had by this point been in print for 17 years. It is line 33 of the original version of Wordsworth's poem 'The Thorn', first published in *Lyrical Ballads* in 1798. It is among the most notorious single lines in all of

Wordsworth's poetry, and one of the lines most often and most extensively discussed by his critics from its first appearance right up to the present moment. Here is the stanza in which the line appears, the third stanza in the poem:

> High on a mountain's highest ridge,
> Where oft the stormy winter gale
> Cuts like a scythe, while through the clouds
> It sweeps from vale to vale;
> Not five yards from the mountain-path,
> This thorn you on your left espy;
> And to the left, three yards beyond,
> You see a little muddy pond
> Of water, never dry;
> I've measured it from side to side:
> 'Tis three feet long, and two feet wide.[39]

Robert Southey, a friend and close literary ally, unsparingly dismissed the poem in his review of *Lyrical Ballads*: 'With that [poem] which is entitled The Thorn, we were altogether displeased.'[40] Coleridge quoted the final couplet of this stanza in *Biographia Literaria* (1817) as a particularly gruesome example of the 'sudden and unpleasant sinkings' which he felt marred Wordsworth's poetry.[41] But, Stephen Parrish swiftly countered, 140 years later, the sinking is all by design: 'the narrator drops' into the 'prosaic detail' of these lines deliberately, in a bold experiment in dramatic monologue.[42] Everything unfamiliarly tedious or idiotic in the poem is nothing but an expert imitation of somebody else's familiarly tedious or idiotic habits of speech. Helen Darbishire thought the whole poem has 'its weak places, its crudenesses, its tiresome redundancies', and that it here and there 'stumbles [...] on the edge of bathos', but that, in the last couplet of this stanza, it 'perhaps tips over' that edge.[43] Geoffrey Hartman described the precision of the lines as 'absurd', but thought that they intensified 'the relentless narrowing of focus' in the poem.[44] The couplet is, for Hartman, a functional element in the careful design of the whole narrative; its local absurdity is subordinate to the overall narrowing of focus and yields up its meaning to it. James H. Averill suggested, yet a little more pleadingly, that the poetically unfamiliar last lines might be a 'parody' of scientific 'exactness'.[45] Wordsworth, then, was parodying science by giving the dimensions of a pond in his poem. More recently, Andrew Bennett has said, as though neutrally just reiterating what is, by this point, the commonly accepted view of the poem, that it is 'famously [...] about conversational ineptitude', and for that reason presumably is not itself inept, and that 'few could take issue with Southey and Coleridge' when they described the poem's impersonation of an old man as 'tedious', though, in fact, not a few critics writing in the past 50 years or so have indeed taken issue with them.[46] Bennett agrees with

Parrish that the triviality is just mimesis of other people's triviality, but, in a sort of implicit homage to Parrish, he thinks the case need now only be assumed and not argued anew.

Wordsworth wrote the lines 'to assist our efforts to visualize' the pond, according to Susan J. Wolfson. It was because, presumably, he thought that we would want to visualize the pond, but that we wouldn't be able to visualize it without knowing its precise dimensions, that Wordsworth gave those dimensions to us 'in assiduous detail'.[47] Wolfson's suggestion would seem to imply that Wordsworth made the great majority of his descriptions of natural objects, which are not given in this sort of assiduous detail, without intending readers to visualize them, or at least without any special care to 'assist our efforts'. Do we, though, in any case, feel that our effort to visualize this pond has been much assisted when we know that it is three feet long, and two feet wide? The previous description, 'little muddy pond', seems to me a better aid to the visual imagination than the measurements in line 33; if anything, the report on its exact dimensions converts the pond from a nearly picturesque image into a mere outline or diagram.

Hugh Sykes Davies suggests, more persuasively, that 'this information was neither funny nor otiose. It was needed to show that the pond was big enough—and only just big enough—for the woman to have drowned her infant in it, and that if she had done so, it must have been a terribly deliberate act; just as the thorn itself was '"[n]ot higher than a two years' child", so that if she had indeed hanged her infant on the tree, it was a gallows of dreadfully fitting height'.[48] That makes sense of the lines as information in a story. The mystery of the poem's narrative depends on hints about what may have happened to the vanished infant; if the pond is exactly infant-size, that surely is a hint that the infant may have been drowned in it. The lines are not, then, funny or otiose; but none of Wordsworth's critics ever said that they were. The thing that upset Coleridge and Southey and Darbishire and others was not that the information in the lines is unnecessary, but that the lines are, unfamiliarly, only information and not poetry. For Coleridge, as for Crabb Robinson, the lines *ought to be* poetry, but were, embarrassingly and unspeakably, 'merely words'.[49] In reply, Wordsworth simply hands the obligation back to his critics: '[T]hey ought to be liked.'

'Wordsworth knew that the terms of his experiment were as difficult as they were radical,' writes Wolfson. '"'The Thorn' is tedious to hundreds," he admits—or perhaps boasts—in response to a friend's displeasure.'[50] Wolfson's 'perhaps boasts' is, I think, probably right. But Wordsworth would not go on for ever boasting that he was in the wrong. 'Wordsworth, who had defended "The

Thorn" for years,' writes Parrish, 'was now ready to abandon the struggle: he revised the poem extensively for the
edition of 1820. The revisions had a single end, to elevate
the language, making it less dramatic and more "poetic".'
What he means and what he doesn't mean by 'poetic',
Parrish doesn't say. He adds, altogether unsatisfactorily:
'[T]he revisions hardly changed the poem.'[51] In all subse-
quent collections of Wordsworth's poetry published
during his lifetime, including the last, published in
1849–50, the third stanza ends:

> You see a little muddy pond
> Of water—never dry,
> Though but of compass small, and bare
> To thirsty suns and parching air.[52]

One thing Parrish could have meant by saying that this
revision was intended to make the poem more 'poetic' is
that Wordsworth had grown unhappy with the original
lines, not for being 'unpoetic' or insufficiently 'poetic' but
for being in some more pressing and active way actually
resistant to 'poetry', or contrary to it. The original lines,
maintained at the significant expense of a strenuous
effort to impose an obligation on his reader (namely, the
real reader who was defined by the certainty that he 'ought
to like' the lines, even if he did not in fact like them),
may in 1820 suddenly—or perhaps at last, after long
and gradually intensifying reflection—have appeared to

Wordsworth no longer to justify the effort of insistence that he must face having to keep up on their behalf. Perhaps whatever was contrary to 'poetry' in the lines no longer seemed contrary in the right way, or was too contrary; or perhaps Wordsworth no longer wished to be the author of lines that were contrary to 'poetry'. Another possibility is that 'poetry', to continue for a moment with Parrish's ambiguous quotation marks, seemed in 1820 more important, or acceptable, than it did in 1798; or in any case, that 'poetry' was no longer something Wordsworth was determined to contradict or resist. If he no longer wished to contradict or resist 'poetry', that may have been because 'poetry' seemed to him no longer to merit, or to elicit resistance, or because he cared for 'poetry' in a new way that seemed irreconcilable with resistance to it, or irreconcilable with being a poet who must tell his reader what he 'ought to like'. 'Poetry' may have emerged with a new meaning, significance or value from the long struggle to impose an obligation: it might be that the effort to oblige his reader to be pleased had been mistaken but not unproductive, since his failure to persuade his reader had instructed Wordsworth in the nature of 'poetry', or its purposes, or its power. Even if Parrish could be right that 'the revisions hardly changed the poem' (I deny that he could), the revisions may nonetheless have changed 'poetry', perhaps even very dramatically; just as, for that matter, the continuation of Wordsworth's resistance to any revision could have changed 'poetry' too.

Parrish's quotation marks are excessively eloquent. I suspect, without his quite meaning it, he encloses the word 'poetic' in a way that opens it to questions that seem liable to multiply indefinitely. The presentation of 'poetic' as if it were a quotation seems on the face of it to be a sort of expressive thrift, as if Parrish were sufficiently confident in being understood by his reader to delegate a part of his argument to punctuation or, rather, to a form of punctuation conventionally adapted to imply authorial disownership of the thought it isolates. The entry for 'quotation mark' in the Oxford English Dictionary (OED) includes the following example from 1795: 'Those lines and ideas which I was conscious, or even suspected, were not my own, are distinguished with quotation marks.' Parrish indicates that 'poetic' is not his own word but one he assigns to Wordsworth (without however directly quoting Wordsworth's use of it); but does he also indicate, or imply, that 'poetic' is not his idea either? In any case, 'poetic' says more than what its word says. Depending on how we decide to literalize the suspension of authorial ownership of the line of argument at this instant, 'poetic' could be a satire against poetry, or against people who misuse or overuse the word, or against anyone who thinks the word could ever be an adequate description of anything, or against Wordsworth; it could also be not a satire but an explanation, even if what it explains is that its word can be no less obscure and no easier to understand when we read it 'in' quotation marks than when we read it out of them or, rather, 'out' of them (since we do not usually think of words not in quotation marks as being out of quotation marks, and so we may like to disown the idea that 'poetic' could ever intelligibly be described as 'out' of quotation marks).

Is this the beginning of a strenuously effortful reading of Parrish's remark, or is it a reading that, to borrow a phrase from much later on in *Phenomenology*, 'vainly and ridiculously strains every nerve to get going' [sich vergeblich und lächerlich abmüht, sich ins Werk zu setzen]?[53] Is this last question, a question about a reading of an interpretation of a revision of a poem by Wordsworth, in any sense also a question about 'The Thorn'? Or even a question which that poem itself asks?

At this point I want to enter the lists and say what none of the critics whose interpretations I have discussed so far has said, that the 1798 couplet—'I've measured it from side to side: / 'Tis three feet long, and two feet wide'—and the second line, line 33, in particular, is the best moment in either version of 'The Thorn', and that the long history of derision, equivocation and apology provoked by this unfamiliarly unpoetic line is proof of its surpassing power. But not just proof: it is the substance of that power, the social history of a confrontational truth. 'To thirsty suns and parching air' is a totally lamentable and nauseating alternative, if lamentation may be done at the same time as nausea. Words that ought to be more than they are, and that ought to be liked but could not be, have been replaced by a wholly unexceptional and famil- iar poeticism that may indifferently enough be 'liked' or not. According to one meaning of the word 'literal', it is a perfectly literal line: it is neither more nor less than what it obviously is. It is 'literal' because it is 'more poetic'. The unfamiliar and disagreeable 1798 line is, by contrast, not at all obviously what it is, or what its author says it is, or what any of its readers has taken it for. The new line must have been accepted by Wordsworth in 1820 because it seemed *right*. If it has had a single good consequence, it is that the sharp contrast it points with the 1798 line shows just how emphatically *wrong* that earlier line must be according to whatever standard of judgement makes the 1820 revision acceptable. If by that standard of judgement the 1820 line is 'more poetic', and is 'literal' by being noth- ing else but what it is, then, by the same standard, the 1798 line (a line not temporally or metaphysically defined until its 1820 replacement condemned it to being 'the original') is poetry that cannot fulfil the concept 'poetry', and is illiteral. Here is a first attempt at a definition of wrong poetry. It is poetry that cannot fulfil the concept 'poetry' and that is illiteral. But note, 'cannot fulfil' the concept does not mean 'will not' fulfil it. 'I've measured it from side to side: / 'Tis three feet long, and two feet wide' is not wrong just by refusing to be right, or by mocking the possibility of being right; as Wordsworth insisted, and insisted passionately for 22 years, the lines 'ought to be liked'. And note further, 'illiteral' does not mean incapable of literalization. It may mean not yet literal, or even 'requiring literalization'.

The familiar and established 1820 substitute is, in my opinion, a good example of language preferred by 'mechanical adoption'. That is, of course, Wordsworth's own famous phrase, from the appendix to his 'Preface' to *Lyrical Ballads*. Here is the passage in which Wordsworth uses it:

> The earliest poets of all nations generally wrote from passion excited by real events; they wrote naturally, and as men: feeling powerfully as they did, their language was daring, and figurative. In succeeding times, Poets, and Men ambitious of the fame of Poets, perceiving the influence of such language, and desirous of producing the same effect without being animated by the same passion, set themselves to a mechanical adoption of these figures of speech, and made use of them, sometimes with propriety, but much more frequently applied them to feelings and thoughts with which they

> had no natural connection whatsoever. A language was
> thus insensibly produced, differing materially from the
> real language of men in *any situation*.[54]

Mechanical adoption may presumably sometimes be instinctive. Psychological and socio-scientific interest in the aetiology of habitual activity was growing steadily at the moment when Wordsworth wrote this 'Preface'. The great modern expositor of mechanical adoption, Maine de Biran, published his long essay *Sur l'influence de l'habitude* in 1803. But the 'Poets, and Men ambitious of the fame of Poets' who are Wordsworth's target did not practice mechanical adoption instinctively; rather, they 'set themselves' to it. E. P. Thompson argued in his 'Disenchantment or Default? A Lay Sermon' that Wordsworth's 'rejection of Godwin was accompanied by a rejection of a mechanical psychology and an abstract enthronement of reason, but not by any rejection of republican ardour'.[55] The rejection of Republican ardour will be our theme before long, but here it seems worth discriminating between 'mechanical psychology' of the sort propounded in eighteenth-century French materialism, whose infamous epitome was De la Mettrie's *L'Homme Machine* (1748), and Wordsworth's carefully satirical observation on the behaviour of 'Poets, and Men ambitious of the fame of Poets' who did not write 'poetry' by mechanical adoption because they were machines full of instincts rather than human beings full of breath and finer spirit but because they calculated that mechanical adoption was the most probable route to social success. They were trying to be right. De la Mettrie and Wordsworth are literalizing in different ways.

But how can this calculated recourse to mechanical adoption be common to 'Poets, and Men ambitious of the fame of Poets'? Does that dissemblingly innocuous 'and' mean that there are poets who, literalized, are nothing but men ambitious of the fame of being what they are? 'The self knows itself as actual only as a *transcended* self,' Hegel wrote in the chapter on 'culture' in the *Phenomenology*.[56] One way to literalize the *Phenomenology* is to raid it for dictums; if we take this sentence—'The self knows itself as actual only as a *transcended* self'—as a dictum, we could disclose the satire in it like this: poets who, 'without being animated by the same passion' as the poet, 'set themselves to a mechanical adoption' of his figures of speech, know themselves as actual poets only as transcendent versions of themselves. Wordsworth does not want to be a transcendent version of himself, or to know himself as that, but to be happy in the very world which is the world of all of us, the place on which in the end we find our happiness, or not at all; except that when this passage from *The Prelude* is done into prose, it is not illiteral enough to make the truth of that hope confrontational. If the poet knows himself as actual only as a *transcended* self, which for the poet who is just a man ambitious of the fame of being what he is means a successful poet, a poet who is right, one of Pound's still sighing but comfortably remunerated 'Fratres Minores', then it is better (meaning that you are really a poet) not to know yourself as actual. Truly being wrong to the point of perdition is a prophylactic against transcendence.

The earliest poets wrote from passion excited by real events. That word 'excited' is one that Wordsworth used with special care. In an earlier prose work he singled out and passionately derided its misuse by Richard Watson, the Bishop of Llandaff. Watson condemned the French Revolution as 'a perturbation [...] *excited* in the minds of the lower orders of the community', as Wordsworth reported him in his 'Letter to the Bishop of Landaff on the extraordinary avowal of his Political Principles contained in the Appendix to his late Sermon by a Republican' (1793).[57] It is a title by a master of line endings. Watson had abandoned the Republican cause in the face of conservative English hostility to the Revolution; that was his self-literalization. Wordsworth, in reply, literalizes Watson's word 'excited' with the use of italics and quotation into what it is. It is what a Wordsworthian reader ought to see: the insinuation that the uprising of 'the lower orders' could not have been spontaneous but that their horror at the condition of their existence must have been stirred up in them, implanted in 'the minds' of their social type, or even that their 'perturbation' was just titillation, an excitement in the mind such as it might owe to pornography. What Republicans believed was the eloquence of suffering was *excited* in their minds: 'in' is a nimble euphemism for 'into'. In the 'Preface', it is the great and most original poets who are excited to passion by what the higher orders of modern men ambitious to sound passionate right now uniformly disregard, that is, by real events. Excitement is not, for Wordsworth 'the advocate of republicanism', as he strenuously names himself in the 'Letter', a disordering of perception induced in suggestible men by other men intent on promoting their own interests, or by events too complex to be understood by political illiterates. Excitement is natural, powerful feeling, and it is precisely when they are no longer animated by it that men shrink insensibly and by degrees into mere right-minded mechanical adopters.

I said that I think the 1798 line in 'The Thorn' is the best line in either version of that poem, that it is a powerfully wrong line, and I described it as words that ought to be more than they are, and that ought to be liked but could not be. This description of line 33 of 'The Thorn' resembles a remark about descriptive language in general by Simon Jarvis in his *Wordsworth's Philosophic Song* (2007):

> The stripping down of poetry, the removal of every-
> thing which is adventitious to a description, all this
> does not in the end leave us with the impossible dead
> letter, with perfected literalness, but rather forces us
> right up against that in language which will not be
> made absolutely literal: the way in which under the
> steadiest description still sounds a prescription, the
> way in which a norm, or a value, or a meaning, echoes
> in what is apparently the most naked and simple 'is'.[58]

This passage in Jarvis' book is prompted by his discussion of the word 'was'. 'Words which speak of nothing more than what we are, when they speak of what we emphatically *are*, must nevertheless speak of more,' Jarvis writes.[59] 'I've measured it from side to side: / 'Tis three feet long, and two feet wide.' These words do not at all obviously speak of what we emphatically *are*. They may not 'be made absolutely literal', but they do seem to be as emphatically literal as Wordsworth or anyone could possibly have made them. Does there resound a prescription in the very literal language of these lines? 'A norm, or a value, or a meaning' covers a lot of bases. Meaning and value can certainly be found in the lines; but can a norm be found in them? Are these notoriously and unfamiliarly stripped down words, words that ought to be more than they are, and that ought to be liked but could not be, incapable of being made absolutely literal because they are covertly normative? I think the answer to that question is a complex 'yes', but I want to differ slightly from Jarvis in my explanation why. To do that I want to return briefly to Sykes Davies' account of 'The Thorn'.

Sykes Davies reminds his readers that

Wordsworth himself [. . .] always attached the highest importance to the poem ['The Thorn'], and regarded an ability to appreciate it properly as the touchstone of the reader who could understand his poetry [. . .] It was a 'favourite' for the best of all reasons, that in the course of writing it, he developed, almost for the first time, what was to become the basic characteristic of his whole handling of words for poetic purposes.[60]

Sykes Davies may well be right that this is why the poem was a favourite of Wordsworth's, or he may be right, at least, that this was the best of all reasons why it should have been. But having a favourite is a complex experience; objects become favourites for reasons other than the best of all reasons. Wordsworth knew that '"The Thorn" is tedious to hundreds,' as he put it, yet for 22 years he *stood by* the poem and insisted that his readers had an obligation to like it. I think he stood by the poem, in fact, all the more obstinately, or even strenuously, the more anxiously and defensively his critics wished to discard it in therapeutic confessions of embarrassment or disgust, and he did that not only because, as Sykes Davies suggests, he had developed in it 'the real language of men' but, more importantly, because the poem was more true for being the object of such protracted hostility and indifference. Wordsworth stood by 'The Thorn' not merely because he liked the poem and wished to deny its upsetting reception, but because he believed in the special social and cognitive importance of loyalty to a despised and derided poem. Its truth was confrontational. Wordsworth is famous for confessing his displeasure at being praised in the wrong way. But he also felt, I think, a very closely related yet distinct pleasure at being dispraised in the right way. He heard a confirmation of the truth of his poetry in the dispraise of it by defensively right-minded readers. I don't suggest that it was easy for him to acknowledge this pleasure, nor that he resisted criticism in a planned and conscious attempt to seek this pleasure out. But it makes sense to me that he should have found truth in the insistence that poetry which even the most sympathetically inclined right-minded judges, and perhaps those judges most especially, cannot like, nonetheless 'ought to be liked'. Perversity in the face of hostile expressions of *Selbsterhaltung* and *das Rechtbehaltenwollen* is a definition of poetic health, something far more deeply interfused than the superficialities of 'poetry'.

What I hear sounded under the confrontationally literal and illiteral language of 'The Thorn' is not the direct echo of a norm or value, exactly, but the echo of an argument about the social and cognitive experience of owning wrong or perverse values and making it a norm to insist on them. Literally, the measurements of the pond are a deeply unfamiliar flourish of *intransigence*; more literally yet, a flourish of an intransigence that once was, and that cannot yet *not* be Republican intransigence. David Bromwich has spotted what he calls a 'republican logic' in another poem in *Lyrical Ballads*, 'Simon Lee'.[61] Evidence of his continuing, increasingly complex and equivocal loyalty to at least the more humanly sympathetic arguments of *The Rights of Man* (1791) and of the French Republicans is not difficult to spot in Wordsworth's poetry of the late 1790s.[62] But what I hear in the measurements of the pond is not Bromwich's Republican logic, nor anything that could convincingly be matched to any sentence in Paine or Rousseau. A more abstract intransigence sounds under the line, an attitude and pressure of conviction dislocated from its social context and its materials of argument, an excitement too powerful to disown that is persisted in with almost nonsensical tenacity. The line is a passionately unfamiliar and wrong line because it does this without conceding the slightest explicit evidence that it is doing it: it cannot be smilingly catalogued as 'Republican intransigence', and yet there that intransigence is, negatively flourished, strenuously non-identical.

If Wordsworth's most notoriously literal line could be made 'absolutely literal', in Jarvis' sense, what would be lost from it? If, that is, the couplet 'I've measured it from side to side: / 'Tis three feet long, and two feet wide' meant nothing but what its words mean (Derrida would object, 'but what are its words?'), how would it be a different couplet? The logic of subtraction was important to Wordsworth, as it was to all 1790s' Republicans. Bromwich calls 'The Thorn' and 'The Idiot Boy' 'an initiation to a power of judging feelings by the standard of sheer humanity'.[63] That is, 'as a Man,' as Wordsworth put it in the 'Preface', 'not as a lawyer, a physician, a mariner, an astronomer, or a natural philosopher' (and as a whole man, not as 'a productive expenditure of human brains, muscles, nerves, hands, etc.').[64] But what did Wordsworth mean in this famous sentence by the word 'Man'? The word so emphatically pronounced is more than the name of what we already know and are; it doesn't name what is already now inalienable, but, in the spirit of Paine, what by now *ought to be* inalienable and what must be legally recognized as such: the sheer humanity we are yet to be allowed, the goal of Republican self-knowledge at the end of the way of revolutionary despair. Wordsworth's universalism in the 'Preface' involves a logic of subtraction: we are men *after* the subtraction of professionalized knowledge and professionalized activity and function, and we are men speaking to men after we stop speaking like professional poets. But after that subtraction we are truly and literally men: *je est un autre* is one literalization too far. 'The poet,' Wordsworth wrote to John Wilson in 1802, 'ought to travel before men occasionally as well as at their sides.' If he is 'a great Poet', he will not be content simply to show men what they already are, but 'he ought to a certain degree to rectify men's feelings, to give them new compositions of feeling'.[65] To be only what I literally am is a blessing that Nature or poetry or revolution may bestow on me; but the poet ought to be more, too: he ought to be not just a man but, occasionally, *the man* who most intransigently insists that we can indeed be just that, even as in uniquely insisting on the possibility he seems to *elevate* himself out of it. Human literalness is outgone by the cognitively and socially transformative act of unfamiliar insistence on it; but only in that radical insistence does it truly shiningly live at all.

What would be lost if the couplet from 'The Thorn' meant only what its words mean is its projection of a social and cognitive necessity. If the couplet were absolutely literal, then its words that ought to be more than they are, and that ought to be liked but could not be, would not be anything but what they are, and nobody would feel any unease or defensive anxiety either in liking or disliking them. They could be, and their replacements from 1820 hereby are, 'smilingly catalogued among their kind'. It was important for Wordsworth not only that this complex power of social and cognitive transformation should resound and unfold in the poem, and that it should resound and unfold in exactly those lines that must seem most improbably and embarrassingly like an inept attempt at absolute literalness, but also that the difficulty of liking them should be felt as strongly and unbearably as anyone could feel it. 'I've measured it from side to side: / 'Tis three feet long, and two feet wide,' writes Wordworth; and the imperious demand repeated to Crabb Robinson in conversation in 1815 is there already in the poem 17 years earlier, implicit in its nearly absolute literalness and its emphatically borderline banal metre and rhyme: ''Tis three feet long, and two feet wide.' You ought to like it, now decide.

The obligation to like a line of poetry may seem like a trivial one, and may seem especially trivial when the line itself can be suspected of making a show of its own triviality; it may even be a hollow obligation. But in the case of this 1798 line from 'The Thorn', what is brilliantly *wrong* is how this apparently trivial or hollow obligation is so tenaciously and so strenuously insisted upon that it *almost* becomes mimetic—which is not quite the same as saying that it becomes negatively mimetic—of a practical revolutionary obligation, a revolutionary obligation of which in any sort of sober reality no right-minded reader could seriously accept that it is mimetic. It ought to be liked because it is literalness and illiteralness passionately insisted upon; but it cannot rightly be liked. It is, rightly speaking, tedious, bathetic and embarrassing. Can this trivial obligation truly be almost mimetic of a revolutionary obligation now pressed out of view? No, I must think, it cannot possibly be, not even almost, because the disproportion is so hilariously immense that the slightest effort to accept that the obligation is mimetic must turn the lines instantly into the worst sort of ersatz alternative to direct political commentary. How, I must think, could anyone in his right mind who cared about politics imagine that he could express a revolutionary obligation by giving the dimensions of a pond? How, for that matter, many readers of poetry today do in fact think, could anyone in his right mind imagine that a poem might exercise any political influence at all? But how else can I possibly begin to like the lines, if not by interpreting Wordsworth's insistence, and my own impression, too, that I am obliged to like them, and by finding in their bid for absolute literalness a dislocated expression of revolutionary thinking and intransigence; and since I already like them, is that not exactly what I must have done? The lines are, of course, about this problem of disproportion. They insinuate a mockery of its complexity by offering the very simple measurements of a pond. But this view of them, that they are about what I have difficulty doing when I read them, seems just as remote from anything their words do, and from any evidence of thematic activity that they unambiguously offer up, as revolutionary obligations seem remote from the trivial obligation to like an unlikeable and jingling couplet.

Absolute literalness may be impossible in language, as Jarvis argues; the human literal, man subtracted to himself and no more, may be impossible in life. But it is part of the power of wrong poetry that not only must it 'speak of more', as Jarvis says, and in so speaking disclose an ontological echo, but the cognitive irreconcilability of emphatic language with absolute literalness must be powerfully and provocatively sounded in it *as a social fact*. It cannot do what, at its most literal and illiteral, it ought to do or must do, but neither can it let go of that necessity and settle reassuringly into emphasis for the sake of emphasis and metaphor for the sake of metaphor: it will be and state the permanent tension between both impossibilities.

Any mere *example* of so improbable a category as 'wrong poetry' will be contentious. Wordsworth's line, in a poem long since smilingly anthologized into a background, may even be an unusually difficult one on which to build a case. I think that it is, and I choose it for that reason, because the speculative category 'wrong poetry' is not merely unstable, counterintuitive or an elicitation of arbitrary human content but it should also be extremely hard to get into any sort of right focus. If it means anything, 'wrong poetry' means just that: a trial of doubt that confounds identification, the perdition of confidence in being right, passionate unease about what will qualify or matter, a compulsion to sublate first reactions under the pressure of sheer insistence on whatever most emphatically escapes them, and irreversible resistance of whatever thought seems most nearly conclusively acceptable or is in any measure already familiar and satisfying. Unlike 'autonomous art' or 'committed art', it is a category with no fixable content. The criterion for belonging to it is to exceed it. It is not the name or conceptual gloss imposed on a corpus of works but an experience seeking out its literal object, an experience that is possible only on condition that its object be the wrong object. Prynne's *Down where changed* and *Word Order* (1989) and John Wilkinson's *Hid Lip* (1992) are among the most compelling sets of poems of the last 40 years to push their way into and define the category as I experience it, only of course for the category then to migrate, shrink or vanish. Prynne and Wilkinson are, in any case, poets who think hard about what it means to be a plaything in the 'game of culture', as Wordsworth did before them, and as none of our present conventional and established Faber poets did before or after them, but who also tax and stretch grammar, idiom, diction,

propositions, echo and utterance to a breaking point in-
conceivable to the modernist imagination for which fragments lie conveniently in wait to be shored against
individual ruin. They are poets in whose work every wrong
turn is a cognitive transformation, back on to the way of
our despair.

Notes

This is a significantly enlarged and revised version of an
essay that appeared in *Textual Practice* 24(4) (2010).

1. Hegel, *Phenomenology*, p. 35. Cf. Ezra Pound's satirical
   poem 'Fratres Minores', in which our minor brothers in the
   versifying trade 'with minds still hovering above their tes-
   ticles' are caught sighing 'over established and natural fact
   / Long since fully discussed by Ovid' [*Personae* (Lea Baech-
   ler and A. Walton Litz eds) (London: Faber, 1990), p. 78].

2. Hegel, *Phenomenology*, p. 35 (translation emended: following other recent commentators, I adopt 'concept' for
   Hegel's 'Begriff' where Miller chose 'notion').

3. I agree with Simon Jarvis that one of the most difficult
   things about the *Phenomenology* is its 'generic indetermi-
   nacy', which I would begin to define as generic complexity or diversity. See Simon Jarvis, 'Spirit Medium: On
   Hegel's *Phenomenology*', *Cambridge Literary Review* 1(2)
   (2010): 157–69. Quoted from p. 167.

4. Hegel, *Phenomenology*, p. 35 (translation emended).
   Hegel, *Gesammelte Werke*, VOL. 9, p. 41.

5. Yirmiyahu Yovel, *Hegel's Preface to the 'Phenomenology of Spirit'* (Princeton: Princeton University Press, 2005), pp. 174–5.

6. I use the word 'therapeutic' to describe an act of explanation (for example, by means of literalization) that clears away suspicion, ambiguity, anxiety and the possibility of insult. I am adapting the word from Martha C. Nussbaum's brilliant and much more richly extensive use of it in *The Therapy of Desire: Theory and Practice in Hellenistic Ethics* (Princeton: Princeton University Press, 1994).

7. William Wordsworth, *Prelude: The 1805 Text* (Oxford and New York: Oxford University Press, 1970), BK 12, lines 142–3.

8. Yovel, *Hegel's Preface*, p. x.

9. 'Immaturity [Unmündigkeit] is the inability to make use of one's understanding without the guidance of another' (Kant, 'What is Enlightenment?', p. 58). Cf. Paul Guyer, who quotes from Kant's notes on his own copy of his *Observations on the Feeling of the Beautiful and the Sublime* (1764): '[N]o abhorrence can be more natural than that which a person has against servitude. On this account a child cries and becomes bitter if it has to do what another wants without one having made an effort to make that pleasing to him. And it wishes only to become a man quickly and to operate in accordance with its own will' [Paul Guyer, *Kant's System of Nature and Freedom: Selected Essays* (Oxford: Clarendon, 2005), p. 127].

10. Samuel Johnson, 'An Inquiry how far Milton has Accommodated the Sound to the Sense', *Rambler* 3(94) (1751); Alexander Pope, untitled article in the *Guardian* 1(78) (1714).

11. Alexander Pope, *The Prose Works of Alexander Pope, Volume 1: The Earlier Works, 1711–1720* (Norman Ault ed.) (Oxford: Blackwell, 1936), p. 94.

12. On the importance of identifying the real target of 'impersonalized statements one might make about human societies', see Raymond Geuss, *Philosophy and Real Politics* (Princeton: Princeton University Press, 2008), pp. 23–9.

13. Cowper, *The Task*, lines 389–96.

14. MA: 25. For an early appearance of this thought in Marx, cf. Karl Marx, *Critique of Hegel's 'Philosophy of Right'* (Annette Jolin and Joseph O'Malley trans.) (Cambridge: Cambridge University Press, 1970), p. 11. For a criticism of Marx's early belief that the order of subject and predicate in speculative propositions could be reversed to produce a materialist dialectic out of Hegel, see Gillian Rose, *Hegel Contra Sociology* (London: Verso, 2009), pp. 52–3. Michael Rosen suggests that the reversal is in any case 'not sufficient to escape from the metaphysics of idealism' [*On Voluntary Servitude: False Consciousness and the Theory of Ideology* (Cambridge, MA: Harvard University Press, 1996), p. 178n34]. Dieter Heinrich traces the graphic image of 'turning thought on its head' back through Hegel to Carl Gustav Jacob Jacobi [*Between Kant and Hegel: Lectures on German Idealism* (David S. Pacini ed.) (Cambridge, MA: Harvard University Press, 2003), p. 110].

15. Marx and Engels, *The Holy Family*, p. 51; Derrida, *Specters of Marx*, p. 218. Whereas W. H. Auden on the other hand believed that '[h]is penis never fully belongs to a man,' [quoted in Arthur Kirsch, *Auden and Christianity* (New Haven: Yale University Press, 2005), p. 29] to which Montaigne long ago supplied the proleptic correction in the spirit of Marx: 'C'est le jouïr, non le posseder, qui nous rend heureux' [Montaigne, *Essais*, BK 1 (Paris: Garnier-Flammarion, 1969), p. 314].

16. V. I. Lenin, *Materialism and Empirio-criticism: Critical Comments on a Reactionary Philosophy* (Moscow: Progress Publishers, 1967), p. 56.

17. Bertolt Brecht's famous *Verfremdungseffekt* is precisely a technique for exposing a too-bourgeois audience to *die fremde* in Hegel sense.

18. 'Had I the courage of my friend, Heinrich Heine, I should call Mr Jeremy [Bentham] a genius in the way of bourgeois stupidity' [Marx, *Capital*, VOL. 1, (Moscow, 1961), pp. 609–10]. Cf. Lukács:

> The bourgeoisie possesses only the semblance of a human existence. A living contradiction must necessarily arise between semblance and reality, for every individual of the bourgeois class, and it is to a great extent dependent on the individual himself whether he pacifies this contradiction using the means of ideological deception that his class constantly presses onto him, or whether this contradiction remains alive within him and leads to him tearing up the deceptive integuments of bourgeois

ideology, either completely or at least in part ('Marx and the Problem of Ideological Decay', p. 133).

19. Hegel, *Phenomenology*, p. 49. The famous expression 'way of despair' (Weg der Verzweiflung) is Hegel's graphic epithet for the progress of knowledge toward its goal, that is, toward 'the point where knowledge no longer needs to go beyond itself, where knowledge finds itself' (ibid., p. 51).

20. Theodor W. Adorno, *Minima Moralia* (E. F. N. Jephcott trans.) (London: Verso, 1987), p. 70; Theodor W. Adorno, *Gesammelte Schriften* (Rolf Tiedemann ed.), VOL. 4 (Frankfurt am Main: Suhrkamp, 2003), p. 78.

21. Walter Benjamin, 'Experience', in *Selected Writings*, VOL. 1 (Marcus Bullock and Michael W. Jennings eds) (Cambridge, MA: Belknap, 2004), p. 4.

22. Theodor W. Adorno, 'Presuppositions: On the Occasion of a Reading by Hans G. Helms', in *Notes to Literature*, VOL. 2 (Rolf Tiedemann ed., Shierry Weber Nicholsen trans.) (New York: Columbia University Press, 1992), p. 97. For the history and theory of 'immanent criticism', see Walter Benjamin, *The Concept of Criticism in German Romanticism* (1920), in *Selected Writings*, VOL. 1. Immanent critique is possible, writes Benjamin, 'if there is present in the work a reflection that can unfold itself, absolutize itself, and resolve itself in the medium of art' (ibid., pp. 159–60). My point in my comment on Adorno is that *Selbsterhaltung* and *das Rechtbehaltenwollen* have the power to eliminate that 'reflection' from the artwork.

23. Hegel, *Phenomenology*, pp. 51, 50.

24. Ibid., p. 49 (translation emended).

25. Ibid., pp. 17, 51.

26. Emerson uses the phrase in his essay 'The Poet' in the context of a passing rhapsody on the advantages of narcotics and alcohol for poets. Drugs and drink are 'auxiliaries to the centrifugal tendency of a man, to his passage out into free space ... they help him to escape the custody of that body in which he is pent up, and of that jail-yard of individual relations in which he is enclosed' [Ralph Waldo Emerson, *Essays and Lectures* (New York: The Library of America, 1983), p. 460].

27. Wordsworth, *Prose Works*, VOL. 1, p. 139. Marx distinguishes between more easygoing experiences of truth and 'die heiße Leidenschaft der Wahrheit', 'the hot passion of truth', in his early 'Debates on the Freedom of the Press' in Marx and Engels, *Collected Works*, VOL. 1, p. 157; MEGA 1.1, p. 145. The 'head of passion' appears in Marx, *Critique of Hegel's Philosophy*, p. 246.

28. Lukács, *Essays on Realism*, p. 144. But note that the English translator of this text unaccountably deletes from it the following sentence in the German original: 'Jeder wirkliche Realismus bedeutet also den Bruch mit Fetischisierung und Mystifizierung. [Every genuine realism means a break with fetishism and mystification]' [Georg Lukács, *Essays über Realismus,* in *Werke*, VOL. 4 (Neuwied and Berlin: Hermann Luchterhand, 1971), p. 274]. The missing sentence should be reinserted after the sentence ending in 'a living inter-relationship between human beings'.

29. Adorno, *Minima Moralia*, pp. 216–7.

30. Hegel, *Phenomenology*, p. 49.

31. On shame, cf. John Wilkinson: 'I've come to believe that shame attaches increasingly to ways of being which resist final translation into objects *out there* and their manipulation [. . .] Shame resides in the remnant, what we have been unable to leave behind or to consume cleanly' ['Mouthing Off', in *The Lyric Touch: Essays on the Poetry of Excess* (Cambridge: Salt, 2007), p. 175].

32. 'The almost insoluble task is to let neither the power of others, nor our own powerlessness, stupefy us' (Adorno, *Minima Moralia*, p. 57).

33. J. H. Prynne, *Poems* (Fremantle: Fremantle Arts Centre; Newcastle upon Tyne: Bloodaxe, 2005), p. 307.

34. 'The decline of giving is today matched by a hardening against receiving. What this adds up to is the renunciation of happiness itself, and it's this renunciation that alone permits men to cling to *their* sort of happiness' [Adorno, *Minima Moralia*, p. 217 (translation emended)]. The German word here translated as 'renunciation' is *Verleugnung*. This is Freud's term, too, as Adorno must surely have known. E. F. N. Jephcott's translation of *Verleugnung* as 'denial' deletes the implicit reference to Freud. On 'real, active men' (as opposed to 'men as narrated, thought of, imagined, conceived') as the proper subject of a materialist philosophy, see Marx and Engels, *German Ideology*, p. 47. Adorno, like Marx before him, has emphatically literalized Hegel's thinking, displacing 'knowledge' from the propositional role of subject and replacing it with 'real, active men'.

35. 'There is no way out of the game of culture; and one's only chance of objectifying the true nature of the game is to objectify as fully as possible the very operations which one is obliged to use in order to achieve that objectification. *De te fabula narratur.* The reminder is meant for the reader as well as the sociologist' [Pierre Bourdieu, *Distinction: A Social Critique of the Judgement of Taste* (Richard Nice trans.) (London: Routledge, 2006), p. 12]. We might add: for the artist, too.

36. Bourdieu, *Distinction*, p. 7. One consequence of this view for poets is that clear-eyed or 'materialist' recognition of the social communicative and invidious functions of 'past' poetical forms is not by itself good enough grounds to abandon them, however obnoxious their history of application, just as the abandonment of form is 'nowhere near enough' to a true sublation of it. The imaginary transcendence of the invidious European history of genre and form by a radically democratic and undifferentiated 'writing' believed in by US Language Poets is, on this view, really an instance of sentimental Freudian 'substitution' or *Nachfolge*.

37. Cf. Hegel: '[P]ure consciousness [. . .] is not a present actuality but exists only for Faith' (*Phenomenology*, p. 296).

38. Thomas Sandler (ed.), *Diary, Reminiscences, and Correspondence of Henry Crabb Robinson*, VOL. 1 (London: Macmillan, 1869), p. 482. I'm grateful to Ruth Abbott for telling me about this passage, and for all our illuminating conversations about Wordsworth.

39. William Wordsworth, 'The Thorn' in William Wordsworth and Samuel Taylor Coleridge, *Lyrical Ballads* (R. L. Brett and A. R. Jones eds) (London: Routledge, 2001), p. 71.

40. Cited in Hugh Sykes Davies, *Wordsworth and the Worth of Words* (John Kerrigan and Jonathan Wordsworth eds) (Cambridge: Cambridge University Press, 1986), p. 39.

41. Samuel Taylor Coleridge, *Biographia Literaria* (George Watson ed.) (London: J. M. Dent, 1993), p. 195.

42. Stephen Maxfield Parrish, '"The Thorn": Wordsworth's Dramatic Monologue' (rev. edn) in M. H. Abrams (ed.), *Wordsworth: A Collection of Critical Essays* (Englewood Cliffs: Prentice-Hall, 1972), pp.75–84. Quoted from p. 77.

43. Helen Darbishire, *The Poet Wordsworth* (Oxford: Oxford Univesity Press, 1962), pp. 43–4.

44. Geoffrey H. Hartman, *Wordsworth's Poetry: 1787–1814* (New Haven: Yale University Press, 1964), p. 141.

45. James H. Averill, *Wordsworth and the Poetry of Human Suffering* (Ithaca: Cornell University Press, 1980), p. 168.

46. Andrew Bennett, *Wordsworth Writing* (Cambridge: Cambridge University Press, 2007), p. 113.

47. Susan J. Wolfson, *The Questioning Presence: Wordsworth, Keats, and the Interrogative Mode in Romantic Poetry* (Ithaca: Cornell University Press, 1986), p. 53.

48. Sykes Davies, *Wordsworth and the Worth of Words*, p. 10.

49. The citation is from Christopher Ricks, *Milton's Grand Style* (Oxford: Oxford University Press, 1963), p. 54.

Ricks wrote of *Samson Agonistes* that it contains phrases 'which ought to be metaphorical' but which are used by Milton 'with a feebleness that keeps them merely words'.

50. Wolfson, *Questioning Presence*, p. 58.

51. Parrish, 'Wordsworth's Dramatic Monologue', pp. 83–4.

52. Ernest de Selincourt (ed.), *The Poetical Works of William Wordsworth*, VOL. 2 (Oxford: Oxford University Press, 1965), p. 241.

53. Hegel, *Phenomenology*, p. 298; *Gesammelte Werke*, VOL. 9, p. 268.

54. Wordsworth, *Prose Works*, VOL. 1, p. 160.

55. E. P. Thomson, 'Disenchantment or Default? A Lay Sermon' in Conor Cruise O'Brien and William Dean Vanech (ed.), *Power and Consciousness*, (London: University of London Press; New York: New York University Press, 1969), p. 150.

56. Hegel, *Phenomenology*, p. 299.

57. Wordsworth, *Prose Works*, VOL. 1, p. 31.

58. Simon Jarvis, *Wordsworth's Philosophic Song* (Cambridge: Cambridge University Press, 2007), p. 29.

59. Ibid., p. 28.

60. Sykes Davies, *Wordsworth and the Worth of Words*, p. 39.

61. David Bromwich, *Disowned by Memory: Wordsworth's Poetry of the 1790s* (Chicago: University of Chicago Press, 1998), p. 99.

62. As Thompson wrote, Wordsworth's 'rejection of Godwin was accompanied by a rejection of a mechanical

psychology and an abstract enthronement of reason, but not by any rejection of republican ardour' ('Disenchantment or Default?', p. 150).

63. Bromwich, *Disowned by Memory*, p. 94.

64. Wordsworth, *Prose Works*, VOL. 1, p. 139. In *The Class Struggles in France*, Marx more witheringly groups together 'the ideological representatives and spokesmen' of the petty bourgeoisie and peasantry, 'their savants, lawyers, doctors, etc., in a word: their so-called *men of talent*' (Marx and Engels, *Collected Works*, VOL. 10, p. 49).

65. Ernest de Selincourt (ed.), *The Letters of William and Dorothy Wordsworth: The Early Years, 1787–1805* (Oxford: Clarendon, 1967), p. 355.

What is called 'Bathos'?

Strangely do the tastes of men differ according to their
employment & habits of life. 'What a nice well that
would be' said a labouring man to me one day, 'if all
that rubbish was cleared off'. The '*rubbish*' was some of
the most beautiful mosses & lichens & ferns, & other
wild growths, as could possibly be seen [. . .] Weeds
have been called flowers out of place.

Wordsworth

It is not so much the being exempt from Faults, as the
having overcome them, that is an advantage to us: it
being with the follies of the mind as with the weeds of
a field, which if destroy'd and consum'd upon the place
of their birth, enrich and improve it more, than if none
had ever sprung there.

Pope

Early on in his recent book *Le Phénomène érotique* (2003),
the French philosopher Jean-Luc Marion complains
about the language we now *use* to talk about love. 'Not
only do we no longer have a concept of love,' he writes,
'but we lack even a word for it.'

'Love' ['Amour']? It sounds like the most prostituted word [mot]—strictly speaking, the word for prostitution; let's spontaneously rehearse its lexicon: one 'makes' love like one makes war or business deals [on fait la guerre ou des affaires], and all that needs doing is to work out with which 'partners', at what price, for what profit, at what rhythm and how often to 'make' it. As for speaking it, thinking it or celebrating it— silence in the ranks. A silence saturated with a grief that pierces through the political, economic and medical idle chatter [bavardage] which would smother and suppress grief in an attempt to reassure us. In this great erotic graveyard, the air is missing whose vibrations would let a single word [parole] resonate.[1]

Marion's cabinet of modern linguistic curiosities is 'bang up to date', or *alamode*, as the needlingly Frenchified jargon of Martinus Scriblerus, the imaginary author of *Peri Bathous*, would have us dunces typologize it; but Marion's theme is an old and familiar one.[2] 'No longer' having a good enough concept is a conventional and established way of not having one. The *bavardage* whose smotherings and suppressions Marion would like us to find intolerable was already about its business of destroying our silence (by saturating it) in the Black Forest in 1926. Heidegger called it 'Gerede'. The English translators of his *Sein und Zeit* (1927), John Macquarrie and Edward Robinson, go for 'idle talk', conjuring, if we like, T. S. Eliot's women 'talking of Michelangelo' only as they 'come and go', smothering the stillness that would allow them to look steadily at their subject, not 'positively making the past their own' but merely, and a little disgustingly, just prattling over a celebrity extract from it, *Michelangelo*.[3] The women come and go like noisy fads. (Whatever truth could be pressed into that thought is much more confrontationally sounded in Beckett's *Come and Go* [1965] than in 'The Love Song of J. Alfred Prufrock' [1915], since as 'the reader' of 'Prufrock' we are not expected to imagine that 'the women' might after all, in the end, be us, dear readers).

Adorno, tangling in 1946–47 with those damagers of life, the bourgeois 'cultivated philistines', who '[require] that a work of art "give" them something', ventriloquizes the litany of the stupefied in the face of difficult art. 'One is just too stupid [dumm], too old-fashioned [altmodisch], one simply can't keep up. . .' Thus 'the language of the nursing home' takes over where the language of 'exuberance', the language that art profoundly and immanently demands, is idly left off.[4] The 'formula' of this nursing-home patter is, Adorno wrote (from his new home in Los Angeles), 'English'. 'Da muß es nach den englischen Formeln relax and take it easy hergehen.'[5] Worse even than the theatrical confession that one is just too stupid is that gruesome use of the beautiful word 'give'. Adopting the more recently *alamode* English formula of the early twenty-first century, we could trade 'give' for 'get out'. What do I *get out* of the artwork? What's *in it for me*? Is there nothing *in it for me*? What this stupefying pushy demand seems implicitly to acknowledge, startlingly, is the possibility that there really is an immanent content to the artwork, even if that content is allowed to be immanent only on condition that it be available to be appropriated without hassle by the canny and defensive consumer.

Prynne, the contemporary English poet least disposed to relax and take it easy, and the best at excoriating our formulas, has said much the same thing as Adorno since *Kitchen Poems* (1968). 'Do what one can, that's / the gas-and-water talk . . .'[6] 'Doing what one can' turns out, in other words, after the ordinary turn of an ordinary prosy enjambment, to be doing only what is misdignified with the name 'essential': life lived according to the model of keeping utility bills down. Where Adorno called on the language of exuberance, Prynne in the 1960s called on the language of ontology to restore us. A poetry carefully enough in charge of the elements of that language, of names like 'is' and 'am' and 'need', could empower us to rise from the *Profund* of 'possessive individualism' and once more gain the blissful seat of 'who we / are'.[7] But it didn't take Prynne's excellently not quite quasi-satirical 'Sketch for a Financial Theory of the Self', or Heidegger or Adorno or Marion, or even modernity, to make poetry, the

language of exuberance or being, collide with and misab-
sorb the unpoetic patter of finance and commerce and
shopping. Pope's lines from 1738 would fall, or so his
'[r]eader led by the hand' might think, almost perfectly
into Martinus Scriblerus' catalogue of absurdities: 'Near
fifty, and without a Wife / I trust that sinking Fund, my
Life.'[8] That sinking Fund: the base going down. The
couplet insinuates its insult against the wife who has not
been acquired by making her the logical alternative to a
tradable life haemorrhaging its value; she is what surely
ought to have been earned on top of the private investment of erotic hope and solitary desire, by the time that
that investment is nearly 50 years old. Can the investment
be credible otherwise?

Neither is the complaint against paltry and trifling
uses of language and their smothering trick originally a
modern complaint. Boileau, in his *Art Poétique* (1674), laid
down as a cardinal rule: 'Toutesfois n'allez pas, goguenard
dangereux, / Faire Dieu le sujet d'un badinage affreux'
('In any case do not, dangerous mocker, make God the
subject of a frightful banter').[9] Sceptical scrutiny even of
jargonistic literary theoretical language itself is a practice
with a long history. Today's delicate despisers of the 'rhi-
zomatic', 'différance', the 'scriptible' or the 'phallus' might
be surprised to know that the innocuously traditional
description of so much of our great English poetry, 'blank

verse', was long ago rejected with disgust as a bit of ugly jargon. Edward Young in his *Conjectures on Original Composition* of 1759 fulminates in pidgin Miltonese:

> *Blank* is a term of diminution; what we mean by blank verse, is, verse unfallen, uncurst; verse reclaim'd, reinthron'd in the true *language of the Gods*; who never thunder'd, nor suffer'd their *Homer* to thunder, in Rhime; and therefore, I beg you, my Friend, to crown it with some nobler term; nor let the greatness of the thing lie under the defamation of such a name.[10]

Young does not say simply that a better word could be found, he says that a word must be found that is noble enough to 'crown' the art; 'blank' is a not a misidentification but a travesty.

This chapter begins with a proliferation of examples of rejected language because I think there may not be any other way to begin thinking about what bathos is. Bathos will not be defined simply by fixing on a conceptual account or a rhetorical figure, or by selecting the single most representative specimen, but, like every speculative construction, it must be thought and experienced socially. There is as yet no satisfying account of bathos.[11] Writing about the grotesque in an essay published in 1855, Baudelaire opted to be categorical: 'There is but one criterion of the grotesque, and that is laughter—immediate laughter.'[12] Otto Fenichel gave a genetic account of boredom. 'It arises when we must not do what we want to do, or must do what we do not want to do [. . .] *something expected does not occur,*' and even, in a moment of wonderfully ersatz-Republican bathos, 'one should not forget that we have *the right to expect* some "aid to discharge" from the external world.'[13] There is no physiologist or psychologist of bathos. Conceptual descriptions of bathos, or definitions of it under the heading of rhetoric (for example, 'ludicrous descent from the elevated to the commonplace in writing or speech; anticlimax') fail to capture the complexity of the word. In fact, that well-known definition from the OED is not only inadequate to the complexity of the word, but, if we accept that bathos is a speculative construction that must be thought and not a property intrinsic to words, the OED definition is simply wrong, and is, in any case, contradicted by all three of the examples given for it under sense 2, most plainly of all by the original example from Pope, as I will show. Bathos is not simply the name for flat, inadequate or ridiculous poetic language, or the descent into it. Already in the case of Scriblerus' original use of the word there belonged to it many more applications and a much broader meaning and significance. I might say, in something like the spirit of Scriblerian irony, that the uses of the word 'bathos' in criticism are sometimes instances of bathos, in one of the many senses already suggested for the word by Scriblerus.

A proliferation of examples, then, to begin to point out the various uses of the idea, and to offer a first hint that what is called 'philosophy' may be unimaginable without it.

In this chapter I will try to explain what bathos is, in two connected passages of argument. First, I will discuss the text in which the English word 'bathos' made its first appearance, *Peri Bathous*, and I will try to provide, not a simple recapitulation of what the imaginary Scriblerus says *Bathos* is, but a close reading of the whole complex satirical invention of the term in that text. Second, I will try to offer my own theoretical account of bathos based on a reading of some passages from a text which I think has much in common with *Peri Bathous*. The text is an early work by Marx and Engels, *The Holy Family*. Any number of texts by Marx might have served, depending on what idea, person, social fact or text we wish to see reduced to bathos. 'Love', for example, is roasted to ashes in the 'Circular Against Kriege' (1846). Kriege, Marx and his friends think, besides using love as a substitute for opium, is responsible for the thought that 'real people are only "symptoms", features of a "movement" that is afoot "in the depths" of a phantom conjured up by thinking.'[14] Kriege's thinking must be literalized through satire; its only confrontational truth is its emptiness. But what is it that makes the enclosure of 'symptoms' and 'movement' and 'the depths' in quotation marks work as a satirical literalization of Kriege's thinking into just another lump of stupefying and ideological language? I choose *The Holy Family* for the discussion in the second half of the chapter because that work is (to the annoyance of some commentators) mostly what might be called, depending on how we wish to value it, either an exercise in pedantic fault-finding with the expressions of its targets the Young Hegelians or a literary criticism of philosophy.

Before I begin on Scriblerus' great treatise, I need to say a little more about why I think the meaning of bathos is a problem, and why the answer is not obvious. Isn't the common objection in the examples I began with an objection to language that is in the wrong place? Marion would presumably not think himself thrown into a 'business graveyard' if he heard the word 'partner' used among businessmen. That is the company the word belongs in, the society in which it sounds right and normal. Prostitution begins for Marion only when the word appears between lovers. Its intrusion into the erotic scene is a rupture of the scene, just as, for Heidegger, the *da* in *Dasein* is the wrong place for *Gerede*. Could Adorno be so merciless in denunciation of 'the language of the nursing home' as to wish it expulsed even from real nursing homes? Is Prynne's 'gas-and-water talk' a travesty of Being even in the mouth of the destitute tenant figuring out how to pay her gas and water bills? Bathos, we might swiftly conclude, is the word for language that forcibly strikes us as being out of place, imposed where it doesn't belong, not welcome, not wanted here: bits of language that we will not allow to be integrated with the scene of language that we find them in. But this apparently simple definition is itself problematic. What does it mean for a word to *belong to* a context of speech or other language use, and when, and under what sort of conditions, does its belonging there end? Can a word ever belong exclusively to any single context? The instinctive identification of words as 'bathos' (and of course, not only words but rhythms, ideas, metrical organizations, titles, punctuation, rhymes and, since concrete poetry, fonts and the whole typography of a poem can be bathetic, to speak only of poems) tells us something about what we want in poems and what we want out of them, or think we do; but why should we want anything in particular in or out of a poem? Why not want anything or everything *in* it?

One last comment before we get to Scriblerus. Critics who use the word bathos have most often used it to describe words or diction, and have usually treated bathos as if it were a sort of fault or decay caused by use but, as we now look at it, inherent in the language itself. Words are spoken about as if they could fall, not only from a high register into a low one but out of their own sense or meaning. Joseph Spence in Part 2 of his *Essay on Pope's Odyssey* (1727) puts this view in a way Scriblerus must surely have understood: 'Words, when they are us'd vulgarly, grow mean: Like other Fashions, when their use is once got among the Populace, they soon begin to be rejected by the politer Part of the World.'[15] It is vulgar use that leads to rejection by 'the World' (that Augustan figure that Yovel's Hegel fills out to 'the world of knowledge', as discussed in Chapter 2). But how does vulgar use cause words to 'grow mean'? If by 'vulgar' Spence means 'widespread' or 'thoughtless' or 'of the lower social orders', why does not every common word in English grow mean? Why is 'and' not bathetic, or 'to'? Why is '   ' not bathetic? Spence says that words grow mean 'Like other Fashions', so the words he has in mind are fashions; but what makes a word into a fashion? It cannot be use alone, since the majority of words used are difficult to imagine as fashions. Does he mean slang, catchphrases, novel idioms, jargon, the stock of Swift's *Complete Collection of Genteel and Ingenious Conversation* (1738)? But those words are, as soon as they appear in society, already mean, as it were; they need not be 'used' into meanness but already in their first appearance they are very often jokes about the pliability, corruptibility or vulgarity of language. If Spence means that words like these are witty at first, but that the more they are used the more obviously

169

wit seems to vanish from them, or to be difficult to get out of them, because people become tired of old jokes, then he makes a familiar observation about the impermanence of comedy. But Spence does not specify that he means slang, jargon or genteel and ingenious words; and in any case, we might think that even those words 'grow mean' only in the sense that their use value diminishes the more widely they are exchanged and the less fashionable their consumers are. That would be a way of aligning the discussion of 'growing mean' very closely with Marx's account of value in the exchange of commodities (it would be a 'Marxist literalization' of Spence's remark), but it won't work for a definition of bathos because, as we shall see, bathos is not a downward trend or fluctuation in value, analagous to the decrease in price of a commodity that is in oversupply. Bathos is an absolute value, a perfect nil. How can words, however vulgarly used, grow mean to the point of perdition, where they have no value at all?

Jonathan Lear makes a similar suggestion to Spence in his recent book *Therapeutic Action* (2003), but adds a philosophical reflection on the relationship of words 'growing mean' to the vicissitudes ineliminable from thinking, and on the task he thinks those vicissitudes confront us with.

> The terms with which we [psychoanalysts] communicate, no matter what they are—'unconscious' or 'ego'

> or 'intersubjectivity' or 'object relations' or 'bad breast'
> or 'play of signifiers'—tend to lose their vibrancy as
> they are passed along in the community. This is the
> entropy of thought: whatever life the concepts might
> have had when they are first being applied in vivid
> psychoanalytic contexts tends to get drained out of
> them, and they get turned more and more into
> slogans. Eventually, the terms get used in place of
> thinking rather than as an expression of it [. . .] The
> entropy of thought is not a problem that can be com-
> pletely avoided. It is endemic to thinking itself. Even
> the phrase 'entropy of thought' can become a cliché.
> So, too, can warnings to avoid it. So, the task for us is
> to bring our concepts to life.[16]

There is much to recommend this energetic passage of
Lear's, not least the faint but clear echo of a Debordian
panegyric to vivid immediacy in expression and Debordian vigilance against the 'recuperation' of concepts into
workable because workaday order. It's true that 'terms get
used in place of thinking rather than as an expression of
it' by acolytes to a theoretical tendency who never test or
bring into question for themselves the adequacy of its
diction, but are satisfied just to recapitulate or 'use' it. But
it is, I think, a convenient fallacy to say, as Spence did and
Lear still does, and incidentally as Ron Silliman has too,
that words *do* these things: that they grow mean, or that
they lose their vibrancy.[17] Words are treated here in the

way that Marx argued ideas are treated in speculative Hegelian philosophy, that is, as the subjects of propositions, as agents and actors, not as predicates, and not emphatically enough as the objects or material of human activity. Food eaten vulgarly does not grow shit, but the scientifically explicable digestive activity of real men makes it so. Spence and Lear could easily protest that they were speaking figuratively and not emphatically when they made words the subjects of propositions, and that, in any case, their emphasis was as much on the simple, practical use of words as it was on the complex lessening of them. What's not clear from their accounts of the decay or drainage of language is how they might speak otherwise than figuratively, or what they would say about language itself if they did. What needs to be explained for the purposes of an essay on bathos is how the misuse or overuse of words, or the appearance of words in contexts they don't belong to, may end in a total loss of 'vibrancy', if it is not by the agency, entropy or decay of the words themselves.

'It will be a very Instructive piece.' With this pleasantly menacing innuendo Pope announced to Swift in a letter of January 1728 the imminent publication of his, or rather Scriblerus', *Peri Bathous: or, Martinus Scriblerus his Treatise of the Art of Sinking in Poetry*.[18] One thing Pope meant, and that he knew Swift would understand, by 'instructive', was that the 'piece' would cause a fiercely acrimonious public fight.[19] Pope not only relished that fight in prospect, he used the opening chapter of *Peri Bathous* to commend himself directly to his victims for starting the fight in reality. '[W]hereas numberless Poets, Cricks and Orators have compiled and digested the Art of *Ancient Poesie*, there hath not arisen among us one Person so publick spirited, as to perform the like for the *Modern*.'[20] That one person, dunces, is risen. Pope knew, of course, that what he tormentingly called 'publick spirit', his quarries and dupes would prefer to call 'malice'. '[T]his little turbulent Creature has endeavoured to decry and calumniate every Author who has excelled him,' wrote John Dennis in the *Daily Journal* in May 1728; and the same year in his *Remarks on Mr Pope's 'Rape of the Lock'*, 'What shall we say of the insipid *Profound* [i.e. *Peri Bathous*]? What shall we say of the fulsome *Dunciad*? Were they not written in perfect Spight to good Sense, to Decency, to Justice, to Gratitude, to Friendship, to Modesty?'[21] An anonymous author, W. A., in an article published in *Mist's Weekly Journal* in June 1728, deplored Pope's 'uncommon Ill-nature' and blamed him for 'Bickerings and Skirmishes' and even 'a barbarous unnatural Civil War'.[22] Even Pope's friend and well-wisher Francis Atterbury, the Bishop of Rochester, regretted in a letter to his son-in-law the 'very improper and troublesome scuffle' that Pope had plunged into by publishing *Peri Bathous* and the *Dunciad*.[23] Pope was not merely unrepentant in the face of these attacks, he was adamant in his purpose and defiantly unconcerned about (or as Jones and Steeves suggest, he was tactically inviting) the stinging replies he knew his satirical 'Institutes' of the 'Rules of our Art' would bring down on him.[24] To Swift he wrote:

> I despise the world yet, I assure you, more than either Gay or you, and the Court more than all the rest of the world. As for those Scriblers for whom you apprehend I would suppress my *Dulness*, (which by the way, for the future you are to call by a more pompous name, The *Dunceiad*) how much that nest of Hornets are my regard, will easily appear to you when you read the Treatise of the Bathos.[25]

The history of this scuffle is well documented elsewhere. I mention it because it is crucial to keep in mind that bathos did not just enter the language in a text that incidentally long ago caused a public altercation, but that Pope invented the term with that specific aim in mind. Bathos was, first of all, even in Pope's preconception of it, an instrument of public attack; once sublimed out of its scene of altercation the word loses almost all of its vibrancy, in Lear's sense. That is an issue not only for philologists but for anyone who uses the word. Its belonging originally to the context of a public altercation is part of its most basic meaning. Forget this and you lose the violent irony of Scriblerus' explanation in Chapter 9 of *Peri Bathous* that 'the main End and principal Effect of the *Bathos* is to produce *Tranquillity of Mind*'. As Scriblerus has already been at pains to explain, what Dennis would protest is his spontaneous rage is *really* nothing of the kind: it is tranquillity of mind, the pleasures of stupefaction.[26] Bathos was not, in 1727, *in* any language whatsoever; it was *put into* language by Scriblerus when he attacked other poets by contributing *Peri Bathous* to the last volume of Pope's *Miscellanies* in 1728.[27]

Bathos in *Peri Bathous* did not mean the same thing as the Greek βάθος. Bathos, or 'the *profund*', is not βάθος; it is 'our βάθος'. 'Our' is a stinging, satirical pronoun. Bathos is βάθος literalized into the English of 'the World' who are a 'nest of Hornets'. *Peri Bathous* is a satire against pretentious, clumsy and opportunistic neoclassicism aimed at 'our' *alamode* epigones of the ancient poets. Our βάθος is not ancient but linguistically innovative, 'fine by being new', as our Guide explains, and 'perfectly agreeable to the present Customs and best Fashions of this our Metropolis'.[28] (Adorno makes much the same satirical use of the possessive pronoun in *Minima Moralia*, Section 139: 'The decline of giving is today matched by a hardening against receiving. What this adds up to is the renunciation of happiness itself, and it's this renunciation that alone permits men to cling to *their* sort of happiness.'[29] Hazlitt confronts the same truth by embracing it: 'It is not happiness, then, in the abstract, which we seek [...] but a happiness suited to our taste and faculties—that has become a part of ourselves, by habit and enjoyment—that is endeared to us by a thousand recollections, privations, and sufferings.'[30] Our happiness will be the subject of the final chapter of this book.) Our βάθος, Scriblerus explains, lies at the bottom of a local 'Track' not 'yet chalk'd out', rather than in the remote regions of Greek to which Scaliger, Bentley and other philologists had discovered 'a plain and direct Road'.[31] Bathos, then, is intended as a bathetic word, βάθος sunk into English, itself the primary instance of the degeneracy it diagnoses. 'Sometimes a single *Word* will familiarize a poetical Idea,' Scriblerus explains.[32]

Bathos is not, in *Peri Bathous*, a 'ludicrous descent from the elevated to the commonplace in writing or speech; anticlimax', as the OED defines it.[33] The OED cites Pope: 'While a plain and direct road is paved to their νψος, or sublime; no track has been yet chalked out to arrive at our βάθος, or *profund*.' In this example, as everywhere in *Peri Bathous*, bathos is not the descent but the destination. Bathos is what we 'arrive at': not a fall, but what is fallen to; not sinking, but what is sunk to. It is not a fluctuation in value, a relative 'growing mean' within the circulation of values, but the absolute value fixed at the bottom. Scriblerus undertakes to lead the wandering 'Genius's of this Age' like Virgil leading an outing of little Dantes on a school trip in our hell, 'by the hand, and step by step, the gentle downhill way to the *Bathos*; the Bottom, the End, the Central Point, the *non plus ultra* of true Modern Poesie!'[34] Neither does this travel on the downhill way begin, as the OED definition says, on an elevation. It begins among Scriblerus' 'dear Countrymen' on their home turf, 'our *Lowlands of Parnassus*'.[35] A descent, yes, and ludicrous surely, but not from the elevated to the commonplace. Bathos is, as Scriblerus says, an offence against common sense; the commonplace is too good for it: '[W]here there is a Triticalness [that is, a trite criticalness] or Mediocrity in the *Thought*, it can never be sunk into the genuine and perfect *Bathos*.'[36] Low value cannot be made into the absolute value nil by means of vulgarization or mere proliferation as fashion. The descent is from the *Lowlands* to the *non plus ultra*. Scriblerus' prey are not the Miltons and Spensers who now and then lapse into mediocrity; they are rather the Blackmores who never scale those middling heights. '[O]ur greatest Adversaries have sometimes descended towards us,' says Scriblerus, speaking of the writers of truly elevated poetry, 'and doubtless might now and then have arrived at the *Bathos*.' Doubtless they might have, now and then, but bathos is not wielded against them by Scriblerus because they do not fit the identity of the real target of his public attack.[37] Bathos is strictly for the loyalists in lowliness. (I think, incidentally, that Geoffrey Tillotson implicitly recognized as much when he wrote, without thinking it necessary to offer an explanation, that 'there is obviously no poetic diction in the *Dunciad*.' Pope categorically cannot be one of the denizens of 'Modern Poesie'.)[38] It is this insistence, repeated throughout the treatise, that makes it not only a mock-aesthetic or mock-rhetorical treatise but a mock-Republican one, too.

The dispute with the OED definition will be focused by a comparison of *Peri Bathous* with criticism that *does* rail at a ludicrous descent from the elevated, by a critic who loves the soarings and triumphs of his target subject, and who, for that reason, deplores his sinkings with a flashing passion unlike anything in Scriblerus' dark *plaisanterie*.

> The *Don Juan* indeed has great power; but its power is owing to the force of the serious writing, and to the contrast between that and the flashy passages with which it is interlarded. From the sublime to the ridiculous there is but one step. You laugh and are surprised that any one should turn round and *travestie* himself: the drollery is in the utter discontinuity of ideas and feelings. He makes virtue serve as a foil to vice; *dandyism* is (for want of any other) a variety of genius.

> A classical intoxication is followed by the splashing of
> soda-water, by frothy effusions of ordinary bile. After
> the lightning and the hurricane, we are introduced to
> the interior of the cabin and the contents of the wash-
> hand basins. The solemn hero of tragedy plays Scrub
> in the farce. This is 'very tolerable and not to be
> endured'.[39]

'From the sublime to the ridiculous there is but one step,'
Hazlitt decides, so that Byron's fall may not seem so epic
or Satanic as he would like it to seem.[40] But Scriblerus'
votaries must go down at a gentler rate than Byron, 'step by
step', one step at a time, one foot after the other. This passage from Hazlitt's magnificent *Spirit of the Age* (1825)
looks like a specimen description of what is now commonly imagined to be bathos in poetry. Everything exalted
tips stupefyingly into something ordinary or abject: classi-
cal intoxication into soda-water, the hurricane into the ornament of the plug hole. But despite the resemblance, this
passage in Hazlitt and the definition of bathos in the OED
are widely different, because Hazlitt is criticizing and prais-
ing not bad *rhetoric*, but—in a tradition that stretches back
beyond Pope's and Scriblerus' age, at least to Dryden's *Essay
of Dramatic Poesy* (1668)—the tragicomic.

A final objection to the OED definition, and to
what I think may be the common idea of bathos, is that
bathos, as *Peri Bathous* conceives it, is possible not only in
language, but, in principle, in any activity or undertaking.

'[T]he *Bathos* is an *Art*,' we are told, and 'reasoning from
the Affinity there appears between Arts and Sciences, I
doubt not but an active Catcher of Butterflies, a careful
and fanciful Pattern-drawer, an industrious Collector of
Shells, a laborious and tuneful Bagpiper, or a diligent
Breeder of tame Rabbits, might severally excel in their
respective parts of the *Bathos*.'[41] Any activity or undertaking, that is, that may be a hobby, pastime or diversion,
for those with nothing better to do than be diverted.
Bathos is for the diligent, but no less for the diligent idler
than for the diligent hack. Scriblerus of course doesn't give
specimens of bathetic rabbit breeding alongside his specimens of bathetic poetry, and the suggestion that bathos is
diversion in general is brought in parenthetically, as a
pleasant idea 'reasoned from Affinity', not as an observation leading to a principle or definition; but the parenthe-
sis of discursive reasoning is not glaringly any more
satirical than the rest of the treatise, and it does seem like
good evidence that Scriblerus intended to blame our modern metropolites for more than just ludicrous rhetoric.

Pope knew, as Scriblerus was not concerned to know,
that future uses of his word 'bathos' would imply a
homage to its creator, no matter how hostile they might
be. In fact, the more hostile they are, the better, since the
implicit acknowledgement of the power of his instrument
of attack in the context of a fierce *ad hominem* reply to *Peri*

Bathous or the *Dunciad* would evidently be the least syco-
phantic acknowledgment possible. This, too, is part of the
basic meaning of the word as it first entered the language.
Its invention was not only an attack but also a sort of dare:
will you, dunces, admit the justice of my satire against you
by taking up the word I invented specially for it, as if to say,
I know you are but what am I? Matthew Concanen did.
His *Supplement to the Profound* (1728) seized hold of the
very means of bathos-production Pope had just published,
the mock treatise, reduplicated it, and tried to produce
examples of bathos from Pope's own poetry.[42] Dennis
turned Pope's word back against him: '[I]n his mimical
Essays he always *sinks* as far below those whom he
endeavours to counterfeit, as the Actions of a Monkey fall
short of those of a Man [. . .] *A. P__E* [Pope] *sinks* as far
below Sir *John Denham*, as the Bottom of *Windsor Forest* is
below the Summit of *Cooper's-Hill*.'[43] Pope was successful
in never lacking for detractors, and more successful yet in
impressing his authorship so deeply on the language of
detraction that even the insults used against him would in
time redound as homages. Bathos was invented with that
future redounding in mind. Its first use is Scriblerian
mock-heroic, performed in the sure and certain expectation of future acknowledgments of Pope's actual heroism.[44]

Bathos was a 'Bottom', 'End' and 'Central Point' of a
'*Depth*' that could be stared into, as well as travelled to.

Scriblerus' guide to conduct is so nicely comprehensive that it even tells the aspiring what sort of eyes they must have. '[H]is Eyes should be like unto the wrong end of a Perspective Glass, by which all the Objects of Nature are lessen'd.'[45] Pope may have borrowed the image from Dryden. Lisideius, one of the symposiasts in Dryden's *Essay of Dramatic Poesy* (1669), ventures to accuse even Shakespeare of setting the glass the wrong way round.

> [I]f you consider the historical plays of Shakespeare, they are [...] so many chronicles of kings, or the business many times of thirty or forty years, cramped into a representation of two hours and an half; which is not to imitate or paint Nature, but rather to draw her in miniature, to take her in little; to look upon her through the wrong end of a perspective, and receive her images not only much less, but infinitely more imperfect than the life: this, instead of making a play delightful, renders it ridiculous.[46]

History may be the right object but, judged by the fashionable French regime of *Des Trois Unitez*, Shakespeare is a ham-fisted bungler with the instrument for looking at it.[47] Clov in Beckett's *Endgame* (1958) makes the opposite mistake, holding the glass the *right* way round, and pointing it straight into the unglaring *profund*.

> CLOV: Things are livening up. [*He gets up on ladder, raises the telescope, lets it fall.*] I did it on purpose. [*He gets down, picks up the telescope, turns it on auditorium.*]

I see ... a multitude ... in transports ... of joy. [*Pause.*]
That's what I call a magnifier.[48]

(Stage instructions in Beckett's plays are no more innocuously italicized than are the names of abstract concepts
like *knowledge* or *Man* in Marx's satires against the Young
Hegelians. The fact that the italicization of stage instructions is *conventional* in the typography of published play
scripts is no argument against that observation but, rather,
a confirmation of it. *Pause.*) The point for Scriblerus, as
for Lisideius and Beckett, is that not only the glass itself
but also the sight at the bottom of the glass is a production. The manipulator of the perspective is the artificer of
the object at the bottom of it. Scriblerus rejects not only
the shrunken object but the swollen one too: 'the Magni-
fying' and 'the Diminishing' are both listed along with
'The Variegating, Confusing, or Reversing' as 'Tropes *and*
Figures' of the bathos in Chapter 10.[49] This point about
production needs to be stressed. Language does not grow
mean or lose its vibrancy through any activity of its own,
despite the poetical uses that may be found for that
explanation. Rather, meanness and deadness are produced
in words by people speaking and writing. (How exactly
that is done, and why when we read a poem what we see
is just deadness, not a raw material from which deadness
can be produced, is the problem I will address in the final
section of this chapter.) To speak figuratively of words

losing their meaning or their beauty is perhaps implicitly to acknowledge (or otherwise to wish) that it is not in my own power (or should not be), no matter how famous I might be, or whatever cosmological or mythopoetic function I conceive for my writing, to prevent or even significantly to retard the large-scale production of deadness in language, so that it feels natural enough to say that language is just doing this, just as it feels natural to say that life ('my' life, even) just goes on. Freud's concept of the id is incoherent except on the basis that strictly rational explanations of human productivity be allowed to terminate in aporia.

In a recent address to a Chinese audience in Guangzhou, Prynne spoke passionately about the poet's special relationship with truthfulness in language.

> The function of truthfulness is curiously and rather specially invested in poets. It's so, pretty much above other artists in other media, because it's quite difficult, in the sense I'm using now, to be truthful if you're holding a paintbrush, or to be truthful if you're practising the flute. There are no doubt forms of essential truthfulness proper to all artistic expression; but human language has a peculiar close relation with the power of language to be mendacious, that is to say to be false, corrupted, lying, depraved and distorted; and that is the normal condition, of course, of human language in most of its daily uses, most especially so now,

> in the condition of the planet at the present time. So
> poets essentially have to learn to stand outside the lan-
> guage which is their medium and understand its cor-
> ruptions, and from its corruptions make some kind of
> temporary, working sense that a reader can share and
> understand.[50]

If this claim about the special investment of the function
of truthfulness in poets seems obnoxious for being irreconcilable with the most acceptable contemporary accounts
of identity, one recourse for the critic who wishes to dis-
pose of it is to literalize it into a displacement of aristocratic fantasy of the sort long ago dissected into economics
by Thorstein Veblen in his *Theory of the Leisure Class*
(1899). Or equally, it could be 'Romanticism', as dismissed
by the US Language Poets. Or equally, it could be a
revenant from Heidegger, not sufficiently excoriated of its
metaphysics. Or equally, it could be an instance of the
'intellectual narcissism' defined by André Green in *Narcissisme de vie, narcissisme de mort* (1983). Any of these options might seem likely to be a literalization in the
direction of a more democratic conception of poetry
and truthfulness than Prynne's. It does them an obvious
injustice to stack them up in a list, as I just did, each one
introduced by the faintly mocking suggestion, badly
enough disguised as unimaginatively repetitive writing,
that they are all equally valid and for that reason may be

indifferently chosen or rejected. Whether any of these options (they are not options, I might protest, but probabilities, or certainties) will succeed in evacuating Prynne's claim, or producing from Prynne's language a specimen of 'ideology', may depend on whether a confrontational form of truth can be discovered whose statement is powerful enough to make Prynne's words 'grow mean', look ridiculous or emerge into deadness. 'The function of truthfulness is curiously and rather specially invested in poets.' What can we do to this sentence? How can it be fixed at the bottom of the hill?

Here is a thought different from Prynne's, but one that may suggest a reason to think that his claim is neither shrunken nor swollen: that it is alive and not dead. The ideal of poetry is that every expressive detail may be made speculative in something like Hegel's sense. Every word must be lived and thought, by a strenuous effort; and of course, not only words but emphases, rhythms, punctuation, rhymes, line breaks and every detail of our experience in reading a poem and living with it must be the object of that effort. That is not the same as saying that poetry 'is' cognitive. Rather, it means that we must become, always and *again and again*, the reader who makes poetry cognitive. I cannot always do that, I am often enough too stupid for it. (Anyone who reads at night before she falls asleep will remember the experience of sliding from focused and concentrated attention to language into a confused and blurred semblance of concentration; and how, or this at least has been my own experience, a text has the strange ability to continue over the threshold of consciousness and into sleep, as if it is still being read: not absorbed, simply, or irrupted into dreamwork, or spoken in a dreaming voice, but read, by a movement of the eyes across its pages; and how there can rise, as if in consciousness, or really there, an anxiety that the text will be forgotten, or a curiosity tinged with panic about where this suddenly almost autonomous and self-reading text has veered away to, and how I will possibly get back to where I was, to my life in this text before the threshold of sleep, if I can find it. I don't want to lose my place. This dreamwork does not feel like work; it feels anxiously like work not being done. It is always a surprising experience, or has been for me, because it feels as if a voice that is not simply my voice from what must surely now be another world, for now at least, has been carried over into a scene of language that now seems, suddenly and oddly, defined by the anxiety to keep that once waking voice alive, to hear it, to remember it, not to let it be only a dream, or give way to oblivion. It feels like a play acted by what I (who am someone else) know I may call 'primary process' and my waking self, a way of losing the script by exceeding it. It is the anxiety not simply of being unable to make the strenuous effort that this text demands, if I love it (across that threshold, possibly I must), but of watching, as if watching, the spectacle of my own effort blur into confusion, then from confusion as if completely effortlessly, even by the beautiful perdition of effort, into anything else at all. Often enough, too, a poem cannot actually be the object of the strenuous effort I make to disclose the life in it (which is, and is not, my life); I make the effort, but it turns out to be an effort that was possible because of the life in a different object, not because of the poem. (I think Frank O'Hara knew this, and is unusual among poets for writing poems that implicitly invite their reader to like them for reasons that may be nothing to do with anything their words do; that, of course, is not yet the same as saying that we can like the poems for reasons that are nothing to do with what they are, because if my observation about O'Hara is right, then his poems 'are', in part, an invitation to like them for reasons that have nothing to do with their words.) Whether or not there is an *hors texte* in Derrida's sense is not irrelevant to how I conceive the meaning of that effort, that is, the waking effort to disclose the life in a poem; nor is it irrelevant to how I learn again and again what the object of my effort is, or never finally learn. But my decision one way or another about the existence of an *hors texte* will not assist me in my effort to disclose life in words, unless whatever truth I fix into my answer to that question can be made confrontational.

It might seem at first as though nothing could be so irreconcilable with Pope's view of the poet's responsibilities in language as the idea that the poet should not only understand the corruptions of his medium, as Prynne says he must, but that he should make his sense from those corruptions. But Pope wrote *Peri Bathous*, and *Peri Bathous* is made out of bathos. Scriblerus is at once a plagiarist of the corruptions he diagnoses, and the original producer of them. From the passages of Blackmore, just now for the first time made into a proper raw material by satirical quotation, Scriblerus produces bathos. *Peri Bathous* is Pope's authorship of bathos, both the idea of it and its first ever cabinet of specimen curiosities. The real use of every line of poetry it contains is Pope's production, since what is really useful in the lines is not beauty or truth but the *manifestness of the destitution of beauty and truth.* If there is a distinction to be made between Pope and Scriblerus, it is that the passages of Blackmore are profoundly precious material for Pope. Without them, Pope could never be certain to produce poetry with an absolute value, however fulsomely his friends and reviewers might celebrate him. The fact that the absolute value of Pope's Scriblerus' Blackmore is very aggressively defined as *nil*, as the *non plus ultra* and perfect bottom, can hardly have been an incidental feature of *Peri Bathous* either to Pope or, I expect, to the 'Neverending Blackmore', as Pope called him in the *Dunciad*, who had one year left to live; but more significant for Pope than the quantity of the value that can be made absolute is the fact that any value can be made absolute. Bathos is the speculative concept of the necessity for all expressive language, and for poetry most specially, of the absolute value nil. Whether the existence of that absolute value is also a 'fantasy' or a 'fact', 'ideology' or a 'necessity', depends on what happens when you make the strenuous effort to think it: to look at a poem and make its value nothing.

'What we are combating in *Bauer's* criticism is precisely *speculation* reproducing itself as *caricature* [. . .] Critical Criticism [*kritische Kritik*] [. . .] distorts reality into an obvious comedy through philosophy.'[51] Philosophy, like a telescope, can be set up the wrong way round. The most carefully calculated insult in this remark is Marx's suggestion that he and Engels can have nothing to do with making Bruno Bauer ridiculous, or hollowing out his thinking, because Bauer's own criticism takes care of that all by itself.[52] Critical Criticism 'reproduces itself' in a stupid form: it does not need to be produced. The object of attack is an automaton that turns by mechanical adoption into nothing but the function and meaning that its attackers say it has.

The first chapter of Marx and Engels' *The Holy Family* is a catalogue of the 'unintelligible' phraseology of Young Hegelian philosophers, the so-called Critical Critics. It is a satire not against jargon, which Marx enjoyed and used as much as Pope did, but against philosophers who don't know jargon when they see it, least of all their own.[53] Commentators on *The Holy Family* have mostly been interested in the early sketch of Marx's theory of the historical destiny of the proletariat in Chapter 4 (whose title is strikingly Scriblerian: '"Critical Criticism" as the Tranquillity of Knowledge'), and have mostly seen in the bulk of the book nothing but a string of exercises in needling and lampoon.[54] It is an exceptionally repetitious book, to the point of draining the energy from its satire by too often overdoing it. When the book has been read for its contribution to Marxist theory, it has been found meagre pickings. But I want to suggest in this chapter that Marx's and Engels' catalogue of Young Hegelian speculative curiosities does involve a theoretical achievement of some importance. To do that, I want to think about what it meant for Marx in particular to make a collection of citations from the works of contemporary writers whose reputations he could demolish, what it meant to think of that sort of satirical aggression as 'publick spirited', and what Marx may have learned from repeating his satirical demolitions so unrelentingly. If there is a theoretical achievement in ridiculing specimens of deadness in philosophical language, what is it? What is it for Marxism?

In a long, mocking criticism of Edgar Bauer's German translation of Proudhon's *Qu'est-ce que la propriété*? (1840), Marx and Engels say, in Scriblerian homage to their victim, that 'Critical Criticism' has '[created] the Critical Proudhon through its translation of the real Proudhon'.[55] As so often in Marx's satires, the satirical image is of a miraculous transfiguration. Bauer has not given his German readers the real Proudhon; he has given them 'the Critical Proudhon', Proudhon miraculously transfigured. In 1848, Marx and Engels would say more straightforwardly that German philosophers 'seized on' French socialist literature, 'only forgetting, that when these writings immigrated from France into Germany, French social conditions had not immigrated along with them'.[56] The language of Proudhon is in the wrong place: the world of spirit, scene of miracles and bourgeois consciousness, 'Germany'. Another of the elect, Szeliga, is venerated for making '*mysteries* out of real *trivialities*'.[57] Szeliga and Bauer are not allowed to be 'real, active men'; they are German superheroes, the fantastical 'incarnations' of Critical Criticism, bad speculative thinking personified.[58] Like the

angels in Milton, they are too spiritually fine for the en-
grossments of any world that could be merely *this* one.
'The Critic,' we are told, 'introduces us to the *ball* for the
sake of *the essence of dancing*.'[59]

In these overdone public attacks on his Critical
Critical contemporaries, Marx developed the lineaments
of the great satire that he would later aim at a more
formidable target. The satire against Critical Criticism in
The Holy Family is an early sketch toward Marx's satire
against the bourgeoisie in *Das Kapital*. 'In its mystified
form,' Marx wrote in *Capital*, 'the authors of the dialectic
[the Critical Critics] became the fashion in Germany,
because it [the dialectic] seemed to transfigure and to
glorify the existing state of things.'[60] In the *Communist
Manifesto*, it is the bourgeoisie as a whole class that is
responsible for wholesale transfiguration and glory.
The bourgeosie as a whole class was of course not in any
remotely straightforward sense 'Critical' or 'Hegelian'; it
very likely had little time or tolerance for any sort of 'speculation' except that practised in a rather more robustly
practical way (the bourgeoisie as 'Practical Practitioners')
by 'the speculating finance aristocracy' whose vampirism
in the wake of the July Revolution of 1830 Marx
disgustedly anatomized in *The Class Struggles in France*
(1850). Since I am writing in England in 2010 under the
Conservative–Liberal Democrat coalition government,

whose answer to every criticism of their demolition of the
public sector is that regrettably they have no alternative
since they must urgently deal with the financial mess
which they define as an inheritance from the previous
government but which is, in fact, the triumphant production of today's financial aristocracy (as Marx said, 'the
faction of the bourgeoisie that ruled and legislated
through the Chambers had a *direct interest* in the *indebt-
edness of the state*. The *state deficit* was really the main
object of its speculation and the chief source of its enrich-
ment'), it seems worth quoting from *The Class Struggles
in France*, at risk of distracting us a little from our argument about bathos.

> Since the finance aristocracy made the laws, was at the
> head of the administration of the state, had command
> of all the organised public authorities, dominated pub-
> lic opinion through the actual state of affairs and
> through the press, the same prostitution, the same
> shameless cheating, the same mania to get rich was
> repeated in every sphere, from the Court to the Café
> Borgne, to get rich not by production, but by pocket-
> ing the already available wealth of others. Clashing
> every moment with the bourgeois laws themselves,
> an unbridled assertion of unhealthy and dissolute
> appetites manifested itself, particularly at the top of
> bourgeois society—lusts wherein wealth derived
> from gambling naturally seeks its satisfaction, where
> pleasure becomes *crapuleux*, where money, filth and

blood commingle. The finance aristocracy, in its mode
of acquisition as well as in its pleasures, is nothing but
the *rebirth of the lumpenproletariat on the heights of
bourgeois society.*[61]

The culinary comminglement of money, filth and
blood is a delicacy to rival *Gallerte*. If this passage distracts
from a theoretical account of bathos by conjuring the
spectre of Jeffrey Skilling, it at the same time contributes
something to that account. 'To get rich not by production,
but by pocketing the already available wealth of others.'
Pope was accused by his enemies of precisely that. *Peri
Bathous* was speculation on the productions of others.

The dialectic packed full of dead language by
'Vishnu-Szeliga', as Marx and Engels mockingly reconsti-
tuted their target in *The Holy Family*, is a dreamy
makeover, a fantasy misdignified with the name speculation. The commodity packed full of dead labour makes
over the living reality of labour in the compulsorily
fetishistic vision of consumers living and eating under
capitalism. Both makeovers, the transfiguration of reality
by dead thinking and language and the transfiguration of
commodities by dead human labour, are 'miracles'. But just
as the commodity is not transfigurable into something
other than an object with an exchange value, so the
Critical Critics are not doing something other than
'dialectic'. Dialectic is no more an infallible instrument or

method, for Marx, than 'poetry' is infallibly passionate enough to carry truth alive into the heart for Wordsworth. Both sorts of thinking not only do fail but must. In fact, both must sometimes fail *absolutely*. Bauer's dialectic is, for Marx, dialectic in dead language, dialectic with the absolute value nil. In an essay written in 1938 but withheld from publication, presumably because he did not wish his satirical remark about his opponent in argument to be 'publick spirited', Brecht replied to Lukács's attacks on 'expressionism' with following advice:

> In art there is the fact of failure, and the fact of partial success. Our metaphysicians must understand this. Works of art can fail so easily; it is so difficult for them to succeed.[62]

Brecht decides, at least for the purposes of this argument with Lukács, that failure is a 'fact'. He literalizes failure into fact. Literally, in production and in the hands of readers, works do fail. 'Our' metaphysicians must learn to think this; they must learn that speculation about art lapses into the very formalism that Lukács condemns in expressionism if it is not disciplined by confrontation with practical failure. The magical efficacy of dialectic in the mouths and pens of Critical Critics is incommensurable with reality but it is a fact; the miracle dies on their lips, their confrontation is exclusive to phantoms. Poetic diction does not stop being 'poetic' in a poem by Thomas

Gray, who was Wordsworth's too tendentiously identified target in his 'Preface', or Blackmore, who was Pope's enormously too aggressively identified target in *Peri Bathous*; but the use of 'poetic diction' in their poems is contradictory to what those poets could possibly wish. Its use for Wordsworth and for Pope is that it makes manifest a specific destitution of beauty and truth. Dialectic does not stop being dialectic in the phantasmagoria of Bauer, but its use is not for advancement on the speculative 'way of despair' literalized as history. Rather, it has another use: it makes manifest the destitution of confrontational truth in 'German philosophy'. *The Holy Family* is an effort to make the destitution of confrontational truth blatant and ridiculous.

The Holy Family, then, is a public attack in which Critical Criticism is held up as the *non plus ultra* of speculative philosophy, the *alamode* style in 'metaphysic bathos' (to borrow from Hazlitt a phrase he targeted at Coleridge in 1817).[63] Just as Scriblerus' specimens of bathos in poetry were 'perfectly agreeable to the present Customs and best Fashions' of London, so the speculative dialectic is perfectly agreeable to Marx and Engels' German contemporaries, the German metaphysical representatives of the group mockingly typologized in the *Communist Manifesto* as 'bourgeois socialists', that is, 'philanthropists' and 'humanitarians' who 'want the living conditions of modern society without the struggles and dangers necessarily resulting therefrom'.[64] *Peri Bathous* is a guide or 'primmer' on the agreeable *non plus ultra* of modern poetry.[65] *The Holy Family* is a primer on the agreeable because only vapidly confrontational German philosophy, a philosophy which is the mere semblance of a fight. With obvious, Scriblerian relish, and looking to start a real fight, our guides present us with a textbook problem from Dialectics for Stupefaction 101.

> *Problem.* You must give me the speculative construction showing how man becomes master over animals.
>
> *Speculative solution.* Given are half a dozen animals, such as the lion, the shark, the snake, the bull, the horse and the pug [*der Mops*]. From these six animals abstract the category: *the* 'Animal'. Imagine *the* 'Animal' to be an independent being. Regard the lion, the shark, the snake, etc., as disguises, incarnations, of *the* 'Animal'. Just as you made your imagination, *the* 'Animal' of your abstraction, into a real being, now make the real animals into beings of abstraction, of your imagination. You see that the 'Animal', which in the *lion* tears man to pieces, in the *shark* swallows him up, in the *snake* stings him with venom, in the *bull* tosses him with its horns and in the *horse* kicks him, only barks at him when it presents itself as a *pug* [*in seinem Dasein als* Mops], and converts the fight against man into the mere *semblance of a fight*. Through its *own consistent development, the* 'Animal' is driven, as we have seen in the *pug*, to debase itself to a *mere clown*. When a child or a childish man runs away from a pug,

the only thing is for the individual no longer to agree to play the silly comedy. The individual X takes this step in the most nonchalant way in the world by using his bamboo cane on the pug. You see how '*Man*', through the agency of the individual X and the pug, has become master over *the* 'Animal', and consequently over animals, and in the *Animal as a pug* has defeated the *lion as an animal*.[66]

The ridiculous 'Mops' or *pug* is a good candidate for what Scriblerus calls the 'single Word' used to 'familiarize [the] poetical Idea' of imaginary speculative solutions to real problems of mastery and survival. But why is the pug ridiculous in this scene? Is the pug any more ridiculous than the shark or the bull? Yes and no. Yes, because it is a stupid animal to be afraid of and to run away from, as 'a childish man' does; because it is the form of the abstraction 'Animal' that the stupid philosopher fixes on, with a predictability that can only be groaned at, since it suits him to adopt whatever enemy can most easily be beaten with his magic bamboo cane (the speculative philosopher will 'remain in the right', like Benjamin's 'philistine', by carefully vetting his phantom enemies with his logic of human resources); and because, significantly, the word itself sounds ridiculous in the scene of philosophical language: *der Mops* is in the wrong place, next to the 'speculative solution'. But no, the pug is no more ridiculous than the bull or the shark, because *anything* from the real world, any animal or object or person or social relation, is *absolutely* in the wrong place next to the 'speculative solution'. Not only is this destitution of truth compulsory for all the animals but it is also compulsory for grammar. The use of the present indicative ('You see that the 'Animal', which in the *lion* tears man to pieces, in the *shark* swallows him up'), of the imperative ('Regard the lion') and of the perfect tense ('the *Animal as a pug* has defeated the *lion as an animal*') can only be to make manifest the destitution of any sort of confrontational truth in this absurd language. Every grammatical turn and torque is a way of being rooted to the spot. There can be no way to accept or believe one part of the 'Speculative solution' more than any other part: by, for instance, being more generous than Marx, or modestly doubting your own fitness to be its reader, or thinking that there is something good in everything. Confrontational truth in the passage has the absolute value nil. Speculation as a textbook exercise is bathos.

One theoretical achievement of *The Holy Family* is that it shows that the absolute value nil is a necessity for the historical materialist critique of German philosophical language. The critique of 'German ideology' is not a critique of ideas, simply, or even of writing, simply, but of a language of philosophy in which all the satirical elements are nothing but 'the mere *semblance of a fight*', a language that is absolutely destitute of confrontational truth. This is a theoretical achievement and not simply a stinging exercise in literary criticism (if that is an acceptable distinction), because Marx learned from doing it that his thinking *in all areas and on all questions* required an absolute value nil.

That may sound an unlikely thing for the great theorist of relative value to have believed. Marx was after all a master dialectician whose writings abound with careful descriptions of contradictory social relations and experiences. Religion was not only a deception but also a genuine comfort; free trade was the intensification of dependency and immiseration for the proletariat but it really was 'freedom' for the bourgeoisie; the bourgeoisie was not only a compulsorily deceptive class unfit to be the ruling interest in a civilized society but also the most dynamic class in history and the one responsible for the greatest ever social achievements in demystification, albeit by advancing from the warm fog of mystery into the icy waters of egotistical calculation. Marx everywhere demonstrates that what is of absolutely no value to one class may be of enormous value to another. But—the proletariat had nothing to lose but its chains; human labour in the commodity is not half living, half dead (in Pope's phraseology, it cannot be 'mediocre') but *Gallerte*, irreversibly and totally dead; there is no god and no heaven; there is, emphatically, in this world and not just in logic or fantasy, experience which is the perfected contradiction of life. When I say that I think Marx learned the necessity of an absolute value nil from satirizing the deadness of German philosophical language, I obviously risk being understood to mean that he would never have thought any of these things without writing his early satires on speculative philosophy. I do not mean that. I am not arguing that Marx learned these ideas, or the dialectic that unfolds them, or the social history that led to them, by writing aggressive satire. In any case, it seems meaningless to imagine what Marx might not have thought if he had not written what he did. What I mean is that the early satires on speculative philosophy repeat again and again, tirelessly and unremittingly, *again and again*, the lesson that truth must be confrontational, not the mere semblance of a fight, and that the early satires are themselves attempts at real fights, and that the fight is at its most real, for Marx, when the argument of the enemy is proved to be a refuge for the absolute value nil. Discrediting the enemy is nowhere near enough; what must be demonstrated is the necessity of his extinction. In Pope's terms, an enemy of that kind is bathos, the irremediable *non plus ultra* of modern poetry, against which every type and intensity of critical blow is more or less transcendentally justified, no matter what might be the complaints of his friends about the overdone and extravagant and self-harming asperities of his satire. For Marx it meant, for one thing, that fetishism could not be overcome by a phenomenology of the commodity, by theoretical adoption of the perspective of omniscience, by not caring, or by gradual improvements in living standards. The absolute value of the objectivity of social perception within the single most fundamental object relation under capitalism is nil, for so long as capitalism continues to exist. If we want to realize a genuine 'social relation' in production that does not begin and end in the marketplace but in our flesh and memory and passion and desire, it is not enough to discredit capitalism a little by adjusting it through the introduction of safety nets; capitalism must be destroyed. For Pope as for Marx, satire against a target defined in these terms cannot be extravagant or too aggressive because the absolute value of the object to be attacked (a poem by Blackmore, 'German philosophy', Kriege's 'love', capitalism) is nil. All these objects have other values besides their absolute value, as Marx the master dialectician would counsel. There will always be someone who likes a bit of bathos: by, for example, enjoying the travesty of God into a baker, or liking the image of the sky as linen. Capitalism not only has other values besides absolute nil but it is also the social scene and origin of all available values. But the absolute value nil is the sovereign value because it is the true speculative concept of these objects: it is what our 'strenuous effort' must be trained to realize and bring to life in them, even as their perfect deadness. This cannot be an idea that Marx needed to learn how to think; it is not a complex or difficult idea or one that requires any special or uncommon use of logic. But it is vital to remember—particularly for rationalistic Marxists it is vital—that the 'strenuous effort of the concept' is not strenuous only for cognition but also for acceptance. The necessity really to think and live the absolute value nil is more difficult to accept than it is to think. The strenuous effort of the concept in Marx is in this respect radically unlike the strenuous effort of the concept in the 'Preface' to Hegel's *Phenomenology*: dialectical thinking sinks to a mere mirage of advancement, for Marx, unless there be somewhere on the way of despair a perfected contradiction that cannot be advanced out of by consciousness, thinking or spirit, but that can, and must, *only* be destroyed by social and political revolution. Spirit is stuck in reality, and reality is most real of all where spirit is most profoundly and inoperably stuck. Perhaps the *most* strenuous effort of the concept in Marx's thinking (I may, in fact, mean, in reading Marx) is the effort never to go beyond that perfected contradiction, or disguise it, or forget it, but to learn again and again, by more and more unendurably emphatic repetition, how to insist on it for ever. The growth of the poetical mind beyond perfected contradiction is its social hypertrophy. The effort not merely to tarry where spirit is stuck but to live there is almost unendurably excessive because it is the perfected opposite of excess: no spontaneous overflow beyond this fact, that wage labour is unalterably a fundamental injustice whose 'speculative concept' is the absolute value *nil humanity*.

One of the most compelling criticisms of the Young Hegelians in *The Holy Family* is aimed not directly at the content of their ideas but at the scheme of antithesis which they invent to guarantee that their ideas will always be important and true. Marx repeats the charge again and again, unrelentingly. 'Critical Criticism itself *begets* its *opposite*, the *stupidity of the Mass*.'[67] Bauer and Co. think that they are criticizing ideas belonging to the real masses, but in reality they use 'the Mass' as the abstract category to which all stupid ideas must belong, irrespective of whether anyone besides themselves ever actually had those ideas. The 'Mass' is a Critical Critical invention, a key concept in a 'speculative solution', like the *pug*. Critical Criticism begets its stupid opposite in order schematically to guarantee the truth of its own constructions by antithesis. Its prior commitment to an abstract scheme of antithesis leaves Critical Criticism incapable of submitting its ideas to the test of empirical verification in reality. 'Criticism's urge to produce stupidities is uncommonly powerful,' Marx and Engels pleasantly add, by way of insinuating that their commitment to truth by antithesis runs deep as a repressed sexual instinct in Bauer and Co., whose blindness to reality is sublimely concupiscent.

This is not simply a mistake which Critical Criticism can stop making. Its whole standard of truth, the only standard by which it can judge the necessity of its conclusions, depends fundamentally on a bad speculative abstraction.

> Critical Criticism, which becomes *objective* to itself only in relation to its antithesis, to the Mass, to *stupidity*, is consequently obliged continually *to produce* this antithesis for itself, and Herren Faucher, Edgar and Szeliga have supplied sufficient proof of their virtuosity in their speciality, the *mass stupefaction* [Verdummung] of persons and things.[68]

For Scriblerus, Lisideius and Beckett, not only the telescope but the sight at the bottom of it is also a production. Critical Criticism's icon of stupidity, 'die *Dummheit der Masse*', is a production too, a plaything in the antithesis that prevents empirical objectivity by guaranteeing objectivity in abstract. The crucial difference is not merely that Pope knows this but Bauer and Co. do not; more importantly, it is that Bauer and Co.'s blindness to the ridiculous destitution of truth in their antithesis is the symptomatic expression of a still deeper blindness. They are blind to the reality that what Marx and Engels here call 'stupefaction', that is, in this case, the schematic production of the abstraction 'die *Dummheit der Masse*' for the purpose of guaranteeing through antithesis the objectivity of bourgeois social criticism, is not an attack on mass deception but a justification of it. Marx and Engels are not claiming that the mass is *not* stupid, not directly at least, but only that Critical Criticism implicitly justifies the real 'stupidity' of the mass (which is not native imbecility but conditioned blindness to its own real interests and enemies, a dream of itself from which it must be awoken) by dumping on the public a speculatively constructed account of freedom and justice instead of the historical materialist account that would alone explain what real deception is and who really is doing the deceiving. Marx wrote in his famous 1843 letter to Arnold Ruge, published in the *Deutsch-Französische Jahrbücher*:

> We do not say to the world: Cease your struggles, they are foolish; we will give you the true slogan of struggle. We merely show the world what it is really fighting for, and consciousness is something that it *has to* acquire, even if it does not want to.
>
> The reform of consciousness consists *only* in making the world aware of its own consciousness, in awakening it out of its dream about itself.[69]

The 'true slogan of struggle' seemed to Marx, at the moment when he wrote this letter, to be nothing but 'the semblance of a fight'. Later, he would become more interested in true slogans. But the truth is, the world really is fighting, right now, whatever its equanimity or inertia; the satire is there in reality, it need only be (it must be) disclosed. Critical Criticism gives the true slogan to the foolish mass to help keep 'bourgeois socialists' from waking out of their dream about themselves. To stop them from making confrontation with the difficult world of the class struggle into a spectacle of work not being done, like reading a text across the threshold of sleep.

What is called 'bathos'? Bathos in the language of philosophy, like bathos in poetry, is not a spontaneous pullulation of decay from the kernel of conceptual or expressive language, just natural or entropic; nor is it something that is the production or possession of the original authors of the language nominated as bathetic, the scandalously abused Dunces or Critical Critics. Bathos is speculation on the productions of idiots. It is put into words by the satirist who attackingly discovers to public view the absolute destitution of truth or beauty. Bauer does not know that he is the real producer of his stupid Mass, just as Blackmore enjoys in dreamy unawareness the bliss of making stupid poetry; in a sense that makes them charitable, since both are working for free. But the absolute value of their labour is nil. They are irremediably blind, not indeed to truth, which, as Marx enjoys repeating, they might see in any direction if they looked about them but to the compulsory destitution of truth in the accounts they themselves produce of it. What Pope, Marx and Engels emphatically diagnose when they make the speculative concept 'bathos' out of other people's poetry and philosophy is a specific pathological social type: the person whose account of reality must compulsorily be destitute of truth. For Pope that person had many social guises—the hireling, the dilettante, the fop, the sycophant, the reprobate, the Modern Poet—but underneath them all, at his most terminally profound, a single constitution: apocalyptic moral idiocy. For Marx and Engels the person right at the bottom, for now at least, because right at the top of capital, was the bourgeois. It still is.

Notes

This is a substantially extended and revised version of an essay that was published in *On Bathos* (Sara Crangle and Peter Nicholls eds) (London: Continuum, 2010).

1. Jean-Luc Marion, *Le Phénomène érotique* (Paris: Grasset, 2003), p. 13 (my translation). Cf. Hazlitt: 'The truth of passion keeps pace with and outvies the extravagance of mere language. There are no words so fine, no flattery so soft, that there is not a sentiment beyond them, that it is impossible to express, at the bottom of the heart where true love is. What idle sounds the common phrases, *adorable, creature, angel, divinity,* are!' (*Selected Writings*, VOL. 7, p. 44).

2. *Prose Works of Alexander Pope*, VOL. 2, p. 220. I use the name 'Martinus Scriblerus' rather than 'Alexander Pope',

because I think we should take seriously the pseudony-mous authorship of the mock treatise, since otherwise we may lose sight of its context of production and reception; and also because, as Edna Leake Steeves has shown [in her 'Introduction' to *The Art of Sinking in Poetry: A Critical Edition* (New York: Russell and Russell, 1968), pp. xxiii–xliii], there remains (and will likely always remain) some doubt over the authorship of the text, which is, com-mentators now agree, mostly or almost entirely by Pope but perhaps not exclusively by him. Arbuthnot probably had a hand in it early on, and numerous commentators have taken it for the work of Swift, at least in some small part. I use 'Martinus Scriblerus' in preference to 'Pope' also in homage to Gillian Rose's discussion of the importance of pseudonymy in her essay on Kierkegaard in Chapter 1 of *The Broken Middle* (Oxford: Blackwell, 1992).

3. The phrase 'positively making the past their own' is adapted from Heidegger's introduction: 'In working out the question of Being, we must heed this assignment, so that by positively making the past our own, we may bring ourselves into full possession of the ownmost possibilites of such inquiry' (Heidegger, *Being and Time*, p. 24). That seems, incidentally, as much a Stalinist way of working out the question of Being as a Nazi one, if we want to literalize Heidegger into a political historian after the image of Machiavelli.

4. Adorno, *Minima Moralia*, pp. 216–7; Theodor W. Adorno, *Minima Moralia: Reflexionen aus dem beschädigten Leben* (Frankfurt am Main: Suhrkamp, 2003), pp. 247–8.

5. Ibid., p. 248. Jephcott doesn't translate Adorno's phrase 'nach den englischen Formeln', but gives just 'the watchword is . . .'; neither does he indicate in his version that 'relax and take it easy' is in English in the original. Bits of English language are now commonly used as shorthand for stupefaction in nonconformist German and French poetry, much as bits of French were once used by Pope, though the ventriloquist's accent and vernacular of the dummy have lately become unmistakably American. The best American poetry, like Kevin Davies' and William Fuller's, knows very well how to use American English as if by ventriloquism and from exile.

6. Prynne, 'Die A Millionaire', *Poems*, p. 15. 'Gas-and-water talk' is a pun on so-called gas-and-water socialism, an English municipal reform movement criticized by Lenin (and later revolutionary socialists) for its limited aims and obfuscation of fundamental class antagonisms.

7. Prynne, 'Numbers in Time of Trouble', *Poems*, p. 17. 'Possessive individualism', one of Prynne's targets in *Kitchen Poems* and much of *The White Stones*, was not his own concept but one recently theorized in C. B. Macpherson, *The Political Theory of Possessive Individualism* (Oxford: Clarendon, 1962).

8. Alexander Pope, 'The Seventh Epistle of the First Book of Horace Imitated in the Manner of Dr Swift' (1738), lines 73–4 in *The Poems of Alexander Pope* (John Butt ed.) (London: Routledge, 1992), p. 666. For a commentary on the passage that includes these lines, and on Pope's experience of and thinking about money and language in general, cf.

Tom Jones, *Pope and Berkeley: The Language of Poetry and Philosophy* (Houndmills: Palgrave, 2005), pp. 86–115. Claude Rawson describes part of *The Dunciad* as 'an anthology of poetic offenses every bit as specifically pilloried in the *Art of Sinking in Poetry*' [Claude Rawson, 'Heroic Notes: Epic Idiom, Revision and the Mock-Footnote from *The Rape of the Lock* to *The Dunciad*', *Proceedings of the British Academy 91*: *Alexander Pope; World and Word* (Howard Erskine-Hill ed.) (Oxford: Oxford University Press, 1998), p. 109]. I paraphrase earlier in my sentence from *Art of Sinking in Poetry*: 'I have undertaken this arduous but necessary task, to lead them as it were by the hand, and step by step, the gentle downhill way to the Bathos' (*Prose Works of Alexander Pope*, VOL. 2, p. 186).

9. Nicolas Boileau, *Art Poétique*, BK 2, lines 187–8; Nicolas Boileau, *Art of Poetry and Lutrin* (William Soames and John Ozell trans.) (Richmond: Oneworld Classics, 2008), p. 24. Soames did not translate these lines very literally; the translation given in brackets is mine. For a useful collection of passages in *Art Poétique* more or less directly imitated by Pope, see E. Audra, *L'Influence Française dans l'Œuvre de Pope* (Paris: Librairie Ancienne Honoré Champion, 1931), p. 209ff.

10. Collected in John Barnard (ed.), *Pope: The Critical Heritage* (London: Routledge, 1973), p. 428.

11. An earlier version of this chapter was published in Sara Crangle and Peter Nicholls (eds), *On Bathos* (London: Continuum, 2010). That book is a good beginning in the collective work of defining the concept. Edna Leake

Steeves'introductory account of the genesis, authorship and background of *Peri Bathous*, and her commentary on that text in *Art of Sinking in Poetry: A Critical Edition*, are both excellent. But there is nothing on the history of bathos since Pope, and no literary theoretical account of it.

12. Charles Baudelaire, 'On the Essence of Laughter' in *The Painter of Modern Life and Other Essays* (Jonathan Mayne ed. and trans.) (New York: Da Capo, 1986), p. 157.

13. Otto Fenichel, 'On the Psychology of Boredom' in Hanna Fenichel and David Rapaport (eds), *The Collected Papers of Otto Fenichel. First Series* (London: Routledge, 1954), p. 301. *Some* is excellent.

14. Marx and Engles, *Collected Works*, VOL. 6, p. 45.

15. Barnard, *Pope: Critical Heritage*, p. 199. Cf. William Wordsworth, *The Thirteen-book Prelude* (Mark L. Reed ed.), VOL. 1, BK 11, lines 243–57 (Ithaca: Cornell University Press, 1991), 300, for a psychological reflection on the power of custom to '[prepare] such wantonness / As makes the greatest things give way to least …'

16. Jonathan Lear, *Therapeutic Action: An Earnest Plea for Irony* (London: Karnac, 2003), p. 34. For a more cosmic and banal cover version of this idea, see Heidegger: 'The history of language shows everywhere a universal tendency toward a narrowing and leveling down of the meaning of words […] Leveling down is a kind of privation. Our age of progress itself is one of privation' [Martin Heidegger, *Zollikon Seminars* (Medard Boss ed., Franz Mayr and Richard Askay trans.) (Evanston: Northwestern University Press, 2001), pp. 49–50].

17. Ron Silliman's account—very influential on US Language Poetry and its admirers, of the 'effacement' of the 'signifier' by 'capitalism'—is in 'Disappearance of the Word, Appearance of the World', *The New Sentence* (New York: Roof, 1995). 'What happens when a language moves toward and passes into a capitalist stage of development is an anaesthetic transformation of the perceived tangibility of the word' (ibid., p. 10). I think it is unclear what Silliman means by 'a language', and also what he means by saying (in ostensibly Marxist terms) that a language can move into a 'stage of development'. To be consistent with the historical materialist view of history invoked by his phrase, Silliman would not only have to be able to predict the next 'stage' of language's development after the present, capitalist one, but that 'stage' itself, in order properly to be a stage in Marx's sense, would have to involve a radical transformation of the basic relations of production and consumption of language, presumably the seizure of power (but which power?) by the current producers of language from its current owners. The wayward vignette begins to look like an inadvertent parody of Marx when we consider that language is already, in its current 'stage', everyone's and no one's possession, in the sense that even the most cruelly exploited worker may freely take home from work with her most of the language she produces during her shift (so that she cannot be 'alienated' from language, in Marx's sense), and that even the most powerful and idle members of society are already inescapably obliged to be producers of language and not just its vampire consumers.

18. George Sherburn (ed.), *The Correspondence of Alexander Pope*: *Volume 2, 1719–1728* (Oxford: Clarendon, 1956), p. 468.

19. Richard F. Jones argues that 'Pope wished to use the *Bathos* to provoke attacks which would seem to justify the publication of the *Dunciad*' ['Another of Pope's Schemes', *Modern Language Notes* 35(6) (1920): 351], that is, that he set out deliberately to cause carefully timed offence with the *Art of Sinking in Poetry*, in expectation that the victims of his satire would lash back at him and, so, provide a public pretext for the otherwise unjustifiably cruel *Dunciad*, which had already long been in preparation. Steeves, in her 'Introduction', makes the same suggestion (Pope, *Art of Sinking in Poetry*, p. xlvi).

20. Pope, *Prose Works*, VOL. 2, p. 186.

21. Barnard, *Pope*: *Critical Heritage*, 157, p. 97.

22. Ibid., p. 211.

23. Ibid., p. 227. Complaints about the excessive malevolence of modern satire had been common in English letters since at least the age of Rochester and Dryden. See, for example, Robert Wolseley: 'For Satyre, that most needful part of our Poetry, it has of late been more abus'd, and is grown more degenerate than any other; most commonly like a Sword in the hands of a Mad-man, it runs a Tilt at all manner of Persons without any sort of distinction or reason' ['Preface' to *Valentinian, a Tragedy* (1685) in David Farley-Hills (ed.), *Rochester*: *The Critical Heritage* (New York: Barnes and Noble, 1972), p. 146].

24. Pope, *Prose Works*, VOL. 2, p. 187.

25. Letter to Swift, 23 March 1728, in Sherburn, *Correspondence of Alexander Pope*, p. 480.

26. Pope, *Prose Works*, VOL. 2, p. 205.

27. The OED, sense 1, cites a use of the Greek βάθος in an English sentence in 1638, but the citation clearly shows that βάθος meant to the author of that sentence something entirely different from what 'bathos' means in *Peri Bathous*. Pope's use of *Bathos* in *Peri Bathous* was the first recorded use in English.

28. Pope, *Prose Works*, VOL. 2, pp. 220, 221. *Our* Metropolis, *our* βάθος: Prynne's 'possessive individualism' in its infantility.

29. Adorno, *Minima Moralia*, p. 217.

30. William Hazlitt, *Selected Writings* (Jon Cook ed.) (Oxford: Oxford University Press, 1999), p. 192.

31. Pope, *Prose Works*, VOL. 2, p. 186. The pedestrian track is a metaphor for pedestrian poetry in Abraham Cowley's 1656 'Preface' to his *Poems* (1656). The Pindaric ode, says its great translator into English, is out of 'the common Roads, and ordinary Tracks of *Poesie*' [Cited in Mary Jacobus, *Romanticism, Writing and Sexual Difference: Essays on 'The Prelude'* (Oxford: Clarendon, 1989), p. 166]. Language in decline, says De Quincey, is 'a dirty high-road which all people detest whilst all are forced to use it' ['The Poetry of Pope' (1848) in John E. Jordan (ed.), *De Quincey as Critic* (London: Routledge, 1973), p. 303].

32. Pope, *Prose Works*, VOL. 2, p. 218.

33. OED, sense 2. Whatever may be the meaning of βάθος in Longinus's Greek, neither βάθος nor *Bathos* could have that meaning in Pope's English. Pope's *Bathos* is not

simply a translation from Longinus; it is a satire aimed at pretentious, ignorant use of Greek concepts and pretentious, ignorant appeal to Greek authority (such as Longinus). Incidentally, 'bathos' is not used in the first English translation of Longinus' treatise to appear after the publication of *Art of Sinking in Poetry* (bearing an epigraph from Pope on its title page), William Smith, *Dionysius Longinus on the sublime: translated from the Greek, with notes and observations, and some account of the life, writings and character of the author* (London, 1739). My guess is that Smith couldn't use the word 'bathos' because Pope in *Peri Bathous* had imposed on it a modern meaning too remote from anything in Longinus.

34. Pope, *Prose Works*, VOL. 2, p. 186.

35. Ibid.

36. Ibid., p. 198.

37. Ibid., p. 187.

38. Geoffrey Tillotson, *Augustan Poetic Diction* (London: Athlone, 1964), p. 28.

39. *The Spirit of the Age or Contemporary Portraits* in Hazlitt, *Selected Writings*, VOL. 7, p. 139.

40. For an account of Byron's unconvincing 'diabolism' by a poet who was able to love Byron only in early life, see T. S. Eliot's 1937 essay 'Byron', in *On Poetry and Poets* (London: Faber & Faber, 1957). pp. 193–206. For Eliot, the 'one step' from the sublime Byron to the ridiculous Byron is called adulthood.

41. Pope, *Prose Works*, VOL. 2, p. 196.

42. Barnard, *Pope: Critical Heritage*, pp. 158–62.

43. Ibid., p. 156. 'Sinking' in this sense was not Pope's invention, but no one had yet used it so scandalously or effectively, and Dennis here implicitly acknowledges as much.

44. For a spirited riposte to the tradition of detracting from Pope right up to the 1980s, see Donald Greene, 'An Anatomy of Pope-bashing' in G. S. Rousseau and Pat Rogers (eds), *The Enduring Legacy: Alexander Pope Tercentenary Essays* (Cambridge: Cambridge University Press, 1988). Greene is interested in how his detractors have failed to understand Pope or even to read him, but he is not interested in the uses of those failures. The speculative construction 'Pope' which belonged to Keats, or Coleridge, or Victorian academic partisans of Romanticism is, for Greene, not itself worth anatomizing but straightforwardly just a hallucination that ought to be deleted by readers who know better.

45. Pope, *Prose Works*, VOL. 2, 192.

46. John Dryden, *Essays of John Dryden* (W. P. Ker ed.), VOL. 1 (Oxford: Clarendon, 1900), p. 59.

47. Dryden discusses the three unities in ibid., p. 38.

48. Samuel Beckett, *Endgame* in *The Complete Dramatic Works* (London: Faber & Faber, 1990), p. 106.

49. Pope, *Prose Works*, VOL. 2, p. 205.

50. J. H. Prynne, 'Keynote Speech at the First Pearl River Poetry Conference, Guangzhou, China, 28th June 2005', *Quid* 16 (2005): 7–16. Quoted from p. 13.

51. Marx and Engels, *The Holy Family*, p. 7; Karl Marx and Friedrich Engels, *Werke*, VOL. 2 (Berlin: Dietz, 1962), p. 7.

52. For the first extended account of Bruno Bauer's thinking and a defence against Marx's unquestionably tendentious, opportunistic and overdone satires, see Douglas Moggach, *The Philosophy and Politics of Bruno Bauer* (Cambridge: Cambridge University Press, 2003). Bauer was himself a spirited and aggressive satirist, not least against the very 'Hegel' with whom Marx was determined to lump him together, namely the 'Hegel' of bad because impractical and unhistorical speculative constructions. In particular, Bauer, in his *Posaune des jungsten Gerichts uber Hegel, den Atheisten und Antichristen: ein Ultimatum*, attacked Hegel's use of 'spirit' (*Geist*) as the universal subject for being a personification. Bauer proposes in that text, albeit only in a passing satirical remark, a connection between Hegel's *Geist* and 'the negro [that is, the savage] who abuses or beats his fetish [wie der Neger seinen Fetisch schmäht oder prügelt]' [Bruno Bauer, *Posaune des jungsten Gerichts uber Hegel, den Atheisten und Antichristen: ein Ultimatum* (Leipzig, 1841), p. 67 (my translation)].

53. On Marx's reading in and quotations from Pope, notably from the *Dunciad*, see S. S. Prawer: 'In his abuse of F. Zabel and others [in *Herr Vogt* (1880)] Marx makes a good deal of play with the English term "dunce" [which he took from Pope]' [*Karl Marx and World Literature* (Oxford: Clarendon, 1976), p. 264n83].

54. Cf. Leszek Kolakowski, *Main Currents of Marxism*, VOL. 1 (Oxford: Oxford University Press, 1989), pp. 147–52. Kolakowski recognizes the important theoretical beginnings in the text but disgustedly describes it (much as

Scriblerus' victims disgustedly described *Peri Bathous*) as 'a virulent, sarcastic, and unscrupulous attack [. . .] full of trivial mockery' (ibid., p. 147). Recall Pope: '[T]he main End and principal Effect of the *Bathos* is to produce *Tranquillity of Mind*' (*Prose Works*, VOL. 2, p. 205).

55. Marx and Engels, *Collected Works*, VOL. 4, p. 51.

56. Karl Marx and Friedrich Engels, *The Communist Manifesto* (David McLellan ed.) (Oxford: Oxford University Press, 2008), p. 30.

57. Marx and Engels, *Collected Works*, VOL. 4, p. 56.

58. On 'real, active men' (as opposed to 'men as narrated, thought of, imagined, conceived') as the proper object of a materialist philosophy, see Marx and Engels, *German Ideology*, p. 47; 'Critical Criticism [. . .] appears in the incarnation of Vishnu-Szeliga' (Marx and Engels, *Collected Works*, VOL. 4, p. 54). But cf. Marx, where this early farcical masque is repeated as tragedy: '[T]he characters who appear on the economic stage are but the personifications of the economical relations that exist between them' (MA: 97).

59. Marx and Engels, *Collected Works*, VOL. 4, p. 68.

60. MA: 25.

61. Marx and Engels, *Collected Works*, VOL. 10, pp. 50–1.

62. Ernst Bloch, Georg Lukács, Bertolt Brecht, Walter Benjamin and Theodor W. Adorno, *Aesthetics and Politics* (London: Verso, 1994), p. 74. The translation is by Stuart Hood. Hood eliminates an exclamation mark from the end of the last sentence quoted here, which in the original German is 'Die Werke können so leicht

mißglücken, da sie doch so schwer glücken!' Bertolt
Brecht, *Schriften zur Literatur und Kunst*, VOL. 2 (Frankfurt am Main: Suhrkamp, 1967), p. 117.

63. Hazlitt used the phrase in his review of *Biographia Liter-
aria* in *Edinburgh Review* 28 (1817); cited in Duncan
Wu, *William Hazlitt: The First Modern Man* (Oxford:
Oxford University Press, 2008), p. 222.

64. Marx and Engels, *Communist Manifesto*, p. 33.

65. Pope, *Prose Works*, VOL. 2, p. 202.

66. Marx and Engels, *Collected Works*, VOL. 4, pp. 75–6; Marx
and Engels, *Werke*, VOL. 2, pp. 79–80.

67. Marx and Engels, *Collected Works*, VOL. 4, p. 14.

68. Ibid., pp. 86–7; Marx and Engels, *Werke*, VOL. 2, p. 91.

69. Marx and Engels, *Collected Works*, VOL. 3, p. 144.

Happiness in Writing

for Simon Jarvis

> to speak of happiness one hesitates those awful
> syllables first asparagus burst abscess
>
> Beckett

At the beginning of Part 2 of *Minima Moralia*, Adorno sets out a series of 'precautions for writers'. The most formidable of the 'precautions' is the following complete paragraph.

> Should the finished text [*Arbeit*: 'work'], no matter of what length, arouse even the slightest misgivings, these should be taken inordinately seriously, to a degree out of all proportion to their apparent importance [*Relevanz*]. Affective involvement in the text [*Die affektive Besetzung des Textes*: 'Besetzung' is the technical term in Freud, known to Adorno, which Strachey translates as 'cathexis'], and vanity, tend to diminish all scruples. What is let pass as a minute doubt may indicate the objective worthlessness of the whole.[1]

Readers of Adorno will know to expect impossible demands. The most confounding of all is saved for the last paragraph of *Minima Moralia*, where Adorno at his most

superlatively emphatical, in high prose lyric, denies that
any philosophy may be 'responsibly practised' except that
which demands from philosophers 'the utterly impossible', namely, that they should think from a 'standpoint
removed, even though by a hair's breadth, from the scope
of existence'.[2] A hair's breadth, space enough for a minute
doubt. By the standard of this annihilatingly sublime
ultimatum, to which the most clamorous reply of merely
existing thought is by prescription infinitely mute, the
demand sounded in the precaution to writers that 'what
is let pass as a minute doubt may indicate the objective worthlessness of the whole' seems almost humanly
gentle. I know what I have to do. I should not let even a
minute doubt pass, since the whole value of my work may
depend upon my insight into the content of a minute
doubt. But what makes this demand so formidable is that
it is not an impossibilistic 'demand placed on thought' by
dialectic, a strenuous effort that will go on forever, but a
practical psychological demand whose impossibility may
be endlessly protested but never established.[3] How, practically, should I meet this demand? Or practically meet it?
The demand is even more impractical than it seems on
first reflection, since the experience of doubt, and perhaps
of minute doubts in particular, may itself be doubted. Is
this truly a 'doubt' that I feel about the sentence I wrote,
or am I giving the name 'doubt' to my feeling because I

can more easily delay the end of writing through sheer procrastination if I can claim a mental motive not yet to believe that I have done what I had to do, whatever that was? Am I doubting conveniently, or dubiously? How do I know that what I call a doubt is not really a fear of having nothing more to do? And in any case, or in that case, how do I know if I am a good enough doubter, even at my best? Is 'doubt' itself a speculative concept, one that must be thought into experience? The demand not to let pass a minute doubt is formidable because it threatens to sink the conversations I have with myself and the whole work of my anxiety into a theatrical ersatz of phenomeno-logical method. The very minuteness of the doubt seems to oblige me, as if in punishment for my disposition to identify and measure doubt, to think that my anxiety is an imitation of method. I ought to accept in writing nothing but what I cannot doubt, Adorno demands; objectivity itself depends on the success of this exclusion. I stare at my doubtful sentence, not this sentence I am now writing, but a sentence on this same screen, in this same room, and, under the pressure of my deliberate solicitude for its objectivity, my real, living thoughts dwindle by a strange fashion of forsaking into the mimicry of a Cartesian meditation. Something not right there.

This final chapter is an essay in close-reading doubt. It is also, albeit only incidentally, a specific and limited criticism of the status of doubt in phenomenology. My suggestion is that phenomenology, when it seems to be interpreting doubt, is sometimes really calculating the quantity of doubt; whereas in reality doubt is never a quantity that may be calculated but always an experience that must be interpreted. Descartes and Husserl, and more recently, Michel Henry, all think in behalf of a questionable preconception of indubitability. Indubitability in these authorships too nearly resembles not just the absence of doubt in general, simply, but the specific absence of doubt which we are left with after all 'doubts' have been subtracted (for example, by the adoption of 'truths' instead). For Husserl, 'the essence of the reduced lived experience of perception', that is, the essence of the experience of perception that is left over after the 'phenomenological epoché' has been performed, 'is incompatible with disbelief and doubt [. . .] disbelief and doubt are precluded'.[4] The idea that doubt is available to be precluded seems to me a good example of what Husserl calls 'preconceptions'. Apodicticity is the bathos of speculation.

But this chapter is an essay in doubt, not just a formal criticism of the status of doubt. It is an essay in close-reading the experience of doubt in poetic composition in particular. Can the experience of doubt have an objective appearance? Can it appear on paper? Can it be read? It may look like this:

> seeking knowledge at that time
>
> Have pleas'd me ~~in those times~~; I sought not then
>
> ~~Knowledge, but craved for power~~, & power I found
>
> Far less than craving power

In the reading text of the *Thirteen-book Prelude* established by Mark L. Reed for the Cornell edition, those lines by Wordsworth, no longer with lines drawn through them in Wordsworth's hand, have been folded into these:

> With strong sensations teeming as it did
> Of past and present, such a place must needs
> Have pleas'd me in those times; I sought not then
> Knowledge, but craved for power, and power I found
> In all things; nothing had a circumscribed
> And narrow influence; but all objects, being
> Themselves capacious, also found in me
> Capaciousness and amplitude of mind:
> Such is the strength and glory of our Youth.[5]

Wordsworth's manuscript revisions, adopted at Book 8, lines 599–600 of the *Fourteen-book Prelude* edited by W. J. B. Owen, may not seem to make any important changes to the sense of the lines. Where Wordsworth first wrote 'I sought not then / Knowledge, but craved for power', he later wrote 'seeking knowledge at that time / Far less than craving power'.[6] 'Where' must be understood literally: the later lines of verse are written where the earlier lines of verse already were. The record of this revision is both the confirmation of that order of priority and at the same time its collapse; there now are, as well as lines that are later and earlier, just these lines, the lines in this single place. The earlier lines of verse are in that instant rewritten, and not simply cancelled, by the superaddition of the correcting line, the strikethrough, that deletes them without yet expunging them. For later readers they will be expunged, or so the strikethrough promises, but for their recurrently first reader, Wordsworth, the graphic, horizontal promise of their future expunction must itself be read, over and over again; the promise of the future expunction of the earlier lines reads less doubtfully than a fresh blank would. The strikethrough *reads* like this: 'deleted but not yet expunged; will be expunged in the end'. Verse and correction are not separated onto verso and recto, but they stand in the same physical place on the page in writing. That place itself, a rectangle of paper, becomes differently original and newly capacious by the amplitude of mind exercised in poetic revision.[7] It is a material testimony of strenuous effort. The page is, literally, an 'object' which, 'being [itself] capacious, also found in [Wordsworth] Capaciousness and amplitude of mind'.

The discovery of a new amplitude of mind is a practical, psychological moment. Here the moment comes in the act of revision, the use of a horizontal line to delete syllables, words, verse and sense. The line and the poetry it deletes are in the same hand, if by that expression we mean that we can identify a single author of both the strikethrough and the deleted words, William Wordsworth; but the revising hand moves differently from the hand that it at once overrules and defines as its 'original', and it traces its letters with a different ink (as I described in my last note). In the real moment in writing when they are revised, the lines *are* the new amplitude; they are the growth of a poet's life. Revision is not a straightforward transfiguring leap from one category or judgement into another, for example, from the wrong words into the right words. What happens to the lines from the point of view of their author is that they re-emerge into originality, not simply by being new or right but by emerging from the obscurity of an over-familiar or exhausted doubtfulness into the illumination of a new doubtfulness full of potential happiness. In their revision, which is not just written on the newly capacious object of the page but also spoken and heard with new amplitude inwardly, a promise is articulated: that, for a while at least, or possibly just for now, the lines may be more passionately owned than disowned. No longer 'I sought not then / Knowledge, but craved for power', but, for now at least more assuredly, 'I sought not then / ~~Knowledge, but craved for power~~'.

The new amplitude of mind in revision is a special intimacy of object and mind. It needs looking at closely, because the ideal of intimacy is that every detail should matter, because in every detail there is the potential for happiness. Does every minute detail in this transcription from the *Thirteen-book Prelude* really matter, or do I at least minutely doubt that some details ought not to matter or need not? Is it significant that the end of line 754, 'I sought not then' is, unlike its continuation in line 755, left unchanged in writing, that it is not deleted by a strikethrough, even though its replacement by 'seeking knowledge at that time' assigns it to the set of verse fragments that Wordsworth promises will be expunged in the end? However demandingly doubtful it may have been earlier in writing, was 'I sought not then' not in the moment of revision a significantly doubtful enough fragment to compel Wordsworth to make a graphic promise of its expunction with a strikethrough in his hand? In any case, the inconsistency is not essentially quantitative: 'I sought not then / ~~Knowledge, but craved for power~~' is not doubtful writing subject to a method of reduction whose diacritical logic requires *one more* deletion, a line through its first four words, to complete the progress of doubt, but doubtful writing whose inconsistency is an object of interpretation irreducible to anything like a paralogism or oversight. Or so at least I must prefer to think, if I don't want to diminish the potential happiness in the new amplitude of the revision. If I do want to diminish that potential happiness, I can literalize the revision more despairingly. What remains undeleted can be nothing but an oversight. But other doubts occur. Should this minute detail in the bewildering immensity of the transcriptions of the *Thirteen-book Prelude* be conceived as a *choice* Wordsworth made in writing? Is it evidence, however minute or doubtful, of his *Besetzung* or cathexis of the objective place in writing whose capacity for 'Truth that cherishes our daily life' may be enlarged to a new amplitude by revision?[8]

From the point of view of a verbal criticism narrowly interested in the ambiguity of propositions in language, these questions may seem hyperpreliminary or just circumlocutory, and not yet a description of what might conventionally be called the 'change in sense' that Wordsworth made by his revision. But these questions *are* close reading and not just speculations about what sort of reading is good or legitimate. A conventional reading might point out that Wordsworth's revision suggests discomfort with the statement in the earlier lines, that is, the emphatic statement that he did *not* seek knowledge but *only* craved for power, as though seeking and craving could be entirely distinct, or knowledge and power could be. That reading might add that the later lines are metrically less unwieldy or ambiguous, since the four stresses of 'seeking knowledge at that time' are more easily kept from ambiguously multiplying in utterance than the two stresses that are meant to be in 'I sought not then' (shouldn't there be three stresses, and couldn't there even be four?); but that the enjambment in the later lines is more shocking, since 'seeking knowledge at that time' does not yet describe a lethargy or reluctance in Wordsworth, but suggests rather the opposite, and it's only when the verse turns back into its next beginning and we read 'Far less than craving power' that we understand that the lines are a criticism of his former ardency. We might then say that the metrical shock in the later lines is intended as a slight moral shock, too, and we might go on to speculate from that example about the increasing moralization of verse technique in the later texts of Wordsworth's poem. From there the conventional reading might ramble off distantly in pursuit of an ideological connection between Wordsworth's lines and De Quincey's theory of the two literatures of knowledge and of power, most fully developed in his essay 'The Poetry of Pope' (1848);[9] or more distantly yet, into Foucault, a place in writing where criticism may now metacritically decide that it should find the contemporary test of its professional relevance and accountability. This conventional reading would be close reading too, and importantly close; but how close can it get? Unmenaced by the threat of sinking into the ersatz of phenomenological method, conventional close reading is also free from the obligation to interpret doubt. It looks as if directly and objectively at what there already is. But Wordsworth passionately knew that it is by the interpretation of doubt that intimacy with an object comes closest to potential happiness.

I want to turn to another moment of doubt in the *Thirteen-book Prelude* that from the perspective of the most literal calculation is still more minute.

> They who had fed their childhood upon dreams,
> The Play-fellows of Fancy, who had made
> All powers of swiftness, subtlety, and strength
> Their ministers, used to stir in lordly wise
> Among the grandest objects of the sense
> And deal with whatsoever they found there
> As if they had within some lurking right
> To wield it:—they too, who, of gentle mood,
> Had watch'd all gentle motions, and to these
> Had fitted their own thoughts, schemers more mild,
> And in the region of their peaceful selves—
> Did now find helpers to their heart's desire,
> And stuff at hand, plastic as they could wish,
> Were call'd upon to exercise their skill,
> Not in Utopia, subterraneous fields,
> Or some secreted Island Heaven knows where;
> But in the very world which is the world
> Of all of us, the place on which in the end
> We find our happiness, or not at all.[10]

This famous passage about the great and beautiful optimism felt by Wordsworth and by his contemporaries who lived and fought through the French Revolution ends, in the manuscript transcriptions, like this:

> And in the region of their peaceful selves
> ~~Did now find helpers to their heart's desire,~~
> And stuff at hand, plastic as they could wish,
> Were call'd upon to exercise their skill,
> Not in Utopia, subterraneous fields,
> Or some secreted Island, Heaven knows where;
> But in the very world which is the world
>   where
> Of all of us, the place ~~on which~~, in the end
>   reap
>   [? know]
> We ~~find~~ our happiness, or not at all.[11]

The line both drawn and written through 'on which' at line 726, and the superaddition of 'where', are both metrical corrections. The hypermetricality of the earlier line, its surplus of syllables (11 rather than 10), is deleted in revision: by writing a line through 'on which', Wordsworth promises the expunction of the surplus syllable in the end. The deletion of hypermetricality and the promise of its expunction is also, here, in this place, the deletion of an emphatic literalism about the standpoint of possible redemption. We will, the line in its first form insists, literally be standing on the world when we find our happiness or do not at all find it; and our happiness itself will be found, if at all, on the world. We who were 'call'd upon to exercise [our] skill [. . .] *in* the very world' will in the end, perhaps by virtue of that exercise, perhaps through fidelity to the knowledge that we were 'call'd' to it, find our happiness *on* the place which that very world is. Is the movement from *in* to *on* a progress? These are, as is too often unthinkingly remarked in professional criticism, *my* italics, my own emphatical recomposition of a distinction in meaning. By owning the italics I admit to a minute doubt over the possibility that the distinction is not originally Wordsworth's and that by adding my italics I have travestied it. In that minute doubt, however, there stands an object for interpretation, a demand for strenuous effort issuing as if from Wordsworth's revision and its promise of meaning, an object that I begin more than minutely to lose at the moment when I find in the concept of 'ambiguity' a set of ready protocols for its interpretation.

If I treat this minute doubt as something subtractable from interpretation, either by mere dismissal of it or by submitting it too exclusively to the protocols for interpretation that already belong to the concept of ambiguity, I cease on that instant to interpret the doubt itself. In fact, I cease properly to experience it as doubt at all, and half-consciously begin to treat it as an obstacle to be admitted or cleared away by something like phenomenological method. I choose either to subtract the doubtful object or to add it. But what I want to interpret is not the ambiguity comprised by two alternatives but the doubt in one composition. My text is not the three items 'Of all of us, the place on which, in the end', 'Of all of us, the place where, in the end' and their hypostatic combination in the concept of ambiguity, but the single real text:

> where
> Of all of us, the place ~~on which~~, in the end

The adverb 'where' depends on the verb 'find' in line 727 and hangs above it, doubly suspended in its higher priority in utterance and in its termination of a clause which could not possibly terminate any correct sentence. It is higher in manuscript position too than its emphatically literal ancestor, being written over it; the conjunction 'on which', which Wordsworth has selected to be the culprit of hypermetricality, is pushed lower down by that choice. I say that he selected 'on which' to be the culprit, rather than that he simply noticed that it is, because 'on which' is not the only candidate in the line; in fact, up to and including the moment at which 'on which' appears, the line is not yet bound to turn out, or even likely to turn out hypermetrical, but still flows with the rhythm of a blank verse line. 'Of all of us, the place on which,—'. Wordsworth need only have completed the line with any two monosyllabic words, or any one disyllabic word, in which he could think without too much doubt that there was a single stress. 'Of all of us, the place on which, at last' would have done it; or, if he had a stronger metrical doubt and wanted to interpret it with just a flicker of hyper-metricality, but not by the sharply pronounced hyper-metricality of the line as it first stood, then 'Of all of us, the place on which, finally' might do. The deletion of hypermetricality through the compression of 'finally' into 'fin'lly' might even be desirable for its anxious mimetic suggestion that the end will come, when it does, a little too fast for us not to stumble just a little in it, or not to lapse backward into 'poetic diction' through adopting a metrical device, contraction, from a life that cannot be lived now because it is not ours, or it is gone.

But I think that Wordsworth had a compelling instinct not to do away with the hypermetricality of his line by accepting 'Of all of us, the place on which—' and writing on from there. Why he should have had, not an acceptable because illuminating doubt about the poten-tial in the line as it stood at this point, but an overfamil-iar or too obviously exhaustible doubt about it that he couldn't let pass, is however unclear until the line in its earliest form is given and read complete. The most im-portant part of the line was yet to come. 'Of all of us, the place on which, in the end'—I feel immediately that the most important part of the line is its end. If I try to doubt something about this judgement, all I can find to doubt about it is how unusually confident I am in believing it;

and that throwback of interpretation into reflexivity, I then think, is surely part of what the line means. Its last three words are its most emphatically suspenseful. They are *held* at the end of the line that cannot possibly be the end of the thought. It is not *in the end* enough, but only an incomplete end. 'Of all of us, the place on which, in the end'—. Wordsworth must have doubted whether he could keep these last three words just as they were without abandoning the line to its original hypermetricality, and may have rejoiced in finding for 'on which' a not too disparate alternative, one that would delete the surplus of syllables and, if not too nicely doubted, might even be taken for an equivalent of his original choice: 'where'. In fact, not only is 'where' emphatically not the equivalent of 'on which', as I have argued in saying that the revision deletes an emphatic literalism, but, more significantly and I think disastrously for the line, 'in the end' is nothing like the same utterance in the revised line that it was in the first line. The words are the same, but not the same. Exculpated of its hypermetricality, 'in the end' sinks from being emphatically suspenseful into a mere indicator of suspense. It sinks from suspense in experience to suspense in 'sense'. The new 'in the end' is very nearly the bathos of the old 'in the end'. The syllables, letters, grammar and word order are of course identical, but it is exactly that merely verbal identity between the two uses of the phrase, 'in the end' in the original hypermetrical line and 'in the end' in the finished because corrected line, that threatens to make the revision into a consummation whose meaning is the erasure (by trimming) of amplitude.

What is at stake in this strenuous effort to correct a line of verse in writing, and, earlier on, what was at stake in the effort of the line as it was first written, which was the effort to make a line whose hypermetrical overflow, however doubtful, is more alive than any corrected alternative could be, is happiness itself.

> where
> Of all of us, the place ~~on which~~, in the end
> reap
> [? know]
> We ~~find~~ our happiness, or not at all.

I wrote earlier that I would turn to a moment of doubt that, from the perspective of the most literal calculation, is still more minute than the moment in Book 8 I discussed earlier on. I meant Wordsworth's doubt over the verb in line 727. Each one of the three verbs included in the manuscript transcription of the line is doubted differently. The earliest and first, 'find', is the only one actually deleted, which is to say marked out for future expunction but not yet expunged. The substitute nearest to it in writing, 'know', is not yet unambiguously rejected, but is triply marked out as doubtful by, first, its confinement in brackets together with a question mark (this is an editorial symbol signifying that the word is not clearly legible in the manuscript, and is a conjectural reading: in other words, 'know' may not really be there at all), second, by the fact that, if 'know' really is there (and it is not an erroneous conjecture), Wordsworth never reinforced it by overwriting during revision, but left it in what he must surely have suspected was very probably an illegible form (if it is there, Wordsworth left it there to be doubted, not to be confidently identified), and finally, by its submission beneath a third possibility, 'reap'. That last word, however, which is free of any editorial symbol and is also the highest on what just now begins to resemble a list in writing, does not seem less doubtful for those reasons but is coloured by doubt rising as though collaterally from the fact that the brackets and question mark of 'know' (the editorial explanation of its illegibility) seem unequal to an outright deletion. If 'know' really is there, and the doubt in 'know' is decisively out of proportion with the doubt in 'reap', why is 'know' not simply marked out for expunction in the end, by a strikethrough in Wordsworth's hand? The word 'reap' is also the last that was written, which may suggest, if we take Wordsworth's 'Preface' literally, that this single late superaddition to the line—'reap'—will be carried alive into the heart by passion only if the passion charged with carrying the whole line can be made to accommodate a late substitute, perhaps by remembrance that, as the great opening to Book 11 of the 1805 *Thirteen-book Prelude* teaches, change must be accepted because it is inevitable. 'And yet this passion, fervent as it was, / Had suffer'd change; how could there fail to be / Some change, if merely hence, that years of life / Were going on, and with them loss or gain / Inevitable, sure alternative'.[12] Should I think that, by omitting it from the end of this sentence, Wordsworth considered that no question mark was required, since from 'years of life' onward the sentence may be read in the indicative mood, as if the sentence were teaching me to accept not only that change is inevitable but also that the inevitability of change ought to be beyond question, too; and should I think that by its overflow across three lines of verse this last part of the sentence, beginning from 'years of life' (the sentence did not begin as a question, and will not end as one) seems to distance itself from the words that would make a question out of it, 'how could there fail', and that this distancing from the opening of the question by means of an overflow in versification is testimony of the power of metre to override grammar, in this case by abandonment of the interrogative mood? If metre can override grammar, does that mean that passion may override scepticism?

Far from denying that there is a trivial aspect to this line of questioning, I want to argue that the trivial aspect is important for being trivial. Its trivial aspect is what insures the interpretation of doubt against sinking into a particular aesthetic ideology. I mean the aesthetic ideology which insists that what makes a 'poem' a 'poem' is the fact that no detail in it could be altered without 'the poem' disappearing completely. This bathydialectical idea not only turns 'the poem' into an abstraction that I think the great majority of poets would not recognize (certainly I do not recognize it from my own experience of writing poems) but it also travesties the idea in *Minima Moralia* that I began with, the genuinely difficult idea that 'what is let pass as a minute doubt may indicate the objective worthlessness of the whole'. The difficulty of that idea in *Minima Moralia* is irreducibly a psychological difficulty. It imposes on the writer a demand that promises to make writing into an incessant and unending trial. The idea of the poem that it conjures is of an intense and enduring forcefield of doubtful and potentially doubtful moments in language, any one of which may yet prove to be either the catastrophic undoing of the whole work or the artifice of its redemption. The aesthetic–ideological alternative which may superficially resemble Adorno's thought is, by contrast, psychologically impotent. It imposes no trial on a writer to know that the alteration of a single detail in her work must cause it to be something other than what it is, or to be excluded from the category 'poem'. Neither is there any happiness to be won or strained after in the transcendent security of belonging to a category so dignified that membership of it means ontological unalterability. Happiness in writing is found in the trial of enduring, intense and ineliminable doubt or not at all. Beckett knew that for even longer than did Wordsworth.

What may strike modern readers most forcefully about Wordsworth's line 727, 'We find our happiness, or not at all', is the idea that the happiness we hope to find 'in the end' is *our* happiness. It is normal in contemporary English to 'find happiness', but not to find our happiness. The locution has fallen out of the vernacular. During Wordsworth's life it was not an uncommon locution. Examples are abundant. I will give here just a few, from texts that Wordsworth could have known but that (with the exception of Edward Young's poem) he hardly need have, to help suggest the amplitude of the expression as it was then heard and understood.

From Young's long poem *Night Thoughts on Life, Death and Immortality* (1744):

> And he that would be barr'd capacity
> Of pain, courts incapacity of bliss.
> Heaven *wills* our happiness, *allows* our doom;
> *Invites* us ardently, but not *compels*;
> Heaven but *persuades*, almighty man *decrees*.[13]

From Hugh Blair's *Sermons* (1801):

> Placed as we are, in the midst of so much ignorance
> with respect to the means of happiness, and at the
> same time under the government of a wise and gra-
> cious Being, who alone is able to effect our happiness,
> acquiescence in his disposal of our lot, is the only dis-
> position that becomes us as rational creatures.[14]

From Johnson's *Rambler* (1750):

> It is therefore the business of wisdom and virtue, to
> select among numberless objects striving for our no-
> tice, such as may enable us to exalt our reason, extend
> our views, and secure our happiness.[15]

These three examples are all like Wordsworth's line in
treating *our happiness* as the object of a transitive verb.
Young's 'will', Blair's 'effect' and Johnson's 'secure', though
in many ways differently suggestive from Wordsworth's
'find', all share with that usage by Wordsworth a cognate
grammar of figuration. Our happiness must be gained by
an effortful activity. But whether the specific activity is a
human one, as in the example from Johnson, or a divine,
as Young and Blair would have it, what separates all three
examples from Wordsworth's 'find' is that our happiness is
for them unambiguously an object only in the grammatical sense, whereas the thought that we might 'find our
happiness' irresistibly suggests the possibility that our
happiness is *somewhere* in the way that places, people
and real physical objects are. That would seem to most
eighteenth-century writers of sermons like a pretty but

hardly a heretical thought, provided that *somewhere* was understood to mean heaven, or the suggestion that our happiness is an object in a place was unambiguously figurative, as for example in a sentence like this one by William Gilpin in 1798: 'The love of God consists in keeping his commandments: and if we keep the commandments of God, of course we shall love our neighbour; and shall find our happiness in our obedience.'[16] In this sentence the preposition 'in' is safely neither literal nor inexchangeable; 'through' would do just as well. There is little or nothing to doubt in this sentence by Gilpin, whatsoever we may like to doubt in the thought it expresses. But the Wordsworthian trial of doubt begins when expression must justify its emphatic literalism.

> That God has given us abilities to provide for our preservation, support, convenience, and happiness, we may readily allow; and we shall probably think it our duty to employ them to those ends. The first error we are apt to commit, is to forget that others are constituted and employed in the same manner with ourselves; and that it is not only a cool determination of reason, they should have room given them to exert their abilities, and to make themselves happy, as we do; but that this conduct is necessary to the existence of society, where alone we can find our happiness.

This passage is from the first pages of David Williams' *Lectures on the universal principles and duties of religion and morality* (1779).[17] It was a year that was to figure in *The Prelude* by being negatively invoked: twice Wordsworth describes a moment of experience at which he was not yet nine years old.[18] The end of the last sentence by Williams quoted here may, I think, be the nearest thing to Wordsworth's thought and expression in the famous original line 727 of the *Thirteen-book Prelude* anywhere in eighteenth-century prose. In any case, it is the nearest I have seen. Williams writes 'society', not 'the very world', but the thought is very nearly kindred. Like Wordsworth, Williams allows his sentence to suggest the possibility that our happiness is literally 'somewhere' and that we will literally find it in the way that we find a physical object: a suggestion so astonishing that it virtually overwhelms the other use of 'find' (which may be the meaning of the sentence, or its most prominent and likely meaning, if we want the sentence to be figurative) to mean 'discover by mental effort', as in the expression 'find the answer'. Like Wordsworth, Williams decisively rules out that 'somewhere' could be heaven, unless 'heaven' be society or the very world of all of us. But most kindred of all is the emphatical word 'alone', a word that risks lyricizing an already exceptionally doubtful thought, a word to which the last words in the *Thirteen-book Prelude*, Book 10, lines 709–27 make equally emphatical reply, in lyric solidarity of thought and insistence. Whether this passage was a source for Wordsworth's lines is an intensely interesting question, because the meaning of those lines will be quite different if they intend lyric solidarity with this passage by Williams from what their meaning would be if the solidarity is coincidental. It would tell us something about what solidarity meant to Wordsworth if we could confirm that at this very place in writing he wished to express it.

I start with 'find' rather than 'know' or 'reap', knowing that my discussion so far is exclusive, because I find more potential happiness in that word than in the others. The doubtfulness of 'find' in the single composition

> reap
> [? know]
> We ~~find~~ our happiness, or not at all.

seems to me a less exhausted, less familiar doubtfulness, a more tense and illuminating doubtfulness than I experience from '[? know]' or 'reap'. 'Find' suggests, surely at least a little strangely, or madly, that our happiness is already there, lying in wait to be discovered like an object, like a present for a child on a treasure hunt. 'Find' also hints at a different verb, 'found', and 'found' would be a good choice—we found our happiness on the world—except that it would have created some superficial, irritating uncertainty as to whether Wordsworth had forgotten what tense he was in, and whether he had committed a solecism by using the past tense of 'find' in a future tense construction. Exposure to a diminutive quibble like that would risk distraction from the real doubtfulness of the line, a sinking from the interpretation of doubt into the calculation of ambiguities. But perhaps neither 'find' nor 'found' could seem illuminatingly doubtful enough, because both would make an internal half-rhyme with 'end', which would raise in lines 726–7 the shadow of a musical chiasmus: all—end / find—all. That might seem too neatly almost epigrammatic; it might also threaten to misinterpret, if only minutely, the difficult asymmetry of the human effort of looking and the human object to be found. But 'know' seems plainly ineffective by comparison, since from the sentence with that verb it wouldn't be clear that our happiness must be inordinately and emphatically known rather than merely known in the way that anything may be known through reflection without a change of place or object. Lyric gives way to noise in the expression 'know our', where the potential elision of the two words in utterance would conjure a phantom non-sense word, 'knowour', whose second syllable might be 'wour' (pronounced 'wower'), an ugly noise not least because of the difficulty of restricting it to one stress and keeping it from sounding like the infantilistic 'wawa'. Lyric is too much at stake in this passage to be trifled with by a noise like that. Perhaps, too, Wordsworth thought that 'know our happiness' was doubtless too near to a sexual pun. But 'know our happiness' is overfamiliarly doubtful for another reason, namely, that it is liable to invoke as a philosophical problem the question whether happiness can be known or if happiness in any way exceeds knowledge, opening promptly on to a vista of inquiries into the mutual exceptionality of happiness and knowledge, pleasure and faith, etc. 'Know' could also be used to mean 'experience', as when we say that we know what something is like because we have done it ourselves, but in that case it must be a pun: it couldn't mean 'only' that, it would have to mean understand or comprehend too; and Wordsworth doesn't want a pun here for nearly the same reason that he doesn't want a trivial noise. The line must be unambiguous in its emphatic doubtfulness, or at least it must have a very minimum of ambiguity to it, or else it will set up discord against the whole lyric of ver-itability. 'Reap our' would give a sonic pun on 'power', not much of a pun but too much by far, and in any case a definitely inappropriate meaning. The double *e* sound in 'we reap' may also have seemed unattractive; Wordsworth may even, at a stretch, have disliked the distant half rhyme with 'belief', also a double *e*. But 'reap' is surely altogether overfamiliarly doubtful because it suggests, first, the figure of death who, once summoned and fitted into the image, is obliged by grammar to be ourselves; and second, a reward or payment of dues on the model of exact remuneration, 'you reap but what you sow', which is exactly the calculating objection leveled against Wordsworth's more complex understanding of natural reciprocity by the embittered Coleridge, first in his brilliant, manipulative and morbid 'Letter to Sara Hutchinson' and then in its yet more false and corrupt public recension, 'Dejection: an Ode'.[19] 'Reap' may also have been unacceptable because Wordsworth wrote often about real farming and real peasants, even about real reapers, and he may not have wanted to use the image of agricultural labour in so strictly metaphorical a sense, particularly at such an emphatic moment of his lyric of veritability. The line would imply, very egregiously, that the real language of men's and women's work that had been so much his enduring concern could *in the end* be sublimed into metaphor when the really serious poetic business of uttering truths about our happiness is attempted. The strikethrough in line 720, '~~Did now find helpers to their heart's desire~~', may have sprung from the same impulse: helpers are not metaphorical, Wordsworth may have thought, and least of all should they be made to appear as metaphors in a passage on the great hope roused by the French revolution.

This is the line I love:

We find our happiness, or not at all.

But I love it best of all by reading this:

reap

[? know]

We ~~find~~ our happiness, or not at all.

What I am closely reading in this composition is doubt. Not, of course, nothing but doubt: I am also reading words, grammar, sense, intentions, rhymes, and verse. But the doubt in this composition, more than anything that criticism would conventionally assign to it as its 'sense' or 'meaning', is the object of my effort and my love. I find something of our potential happiness by close reading and interpreting doubt. I find both my own potential happiness, the love for this line that grows and flourishes in me as I learn to speak it in intimacy, a happiness and love found on the literal object of this page in Wordsworth's transcriptions, his great gift to the posthumous world; and also, though I doubt that I am right, I find what I think may be Wordsworth's happiness: an idea about happiness that was his, certainly, but more importantly still, his strenuous effort, his straining after happiness in writing on the passionate trial of enduring and ineliminable doubt. Belief in reality, like belief in happiness, cannot be found on a preconception of indubitability or apodicticity defined as the perfect stilling or absence of doubt. If any experience not only proves this but renews its proof unendingly until death, it is writing (it is loving). Whatever may be true of the discursive construction of identity and its politics in theory, in writing happiness does not come from ontological promiscuity but from ontological fidelity; but this is true only on condition that fidelity in writing be not the opposite of promiscuity, but its sublime. Fidelity is also more powerfully doubtful than promiscuity, as Wordsworth knew for longer even than Beckett. Fidelity is the element in which doubt is hardest struck by passion.

What is most real to me is what I most passionately doubt.

~~*Kein Glück ohne Fetischismus.*~~

Notes

This essay was published in *World Picture* 3 (2009) and is reprinted here with the author's permission.

1. Adorno, *Minima Moralia*, p. 85; Adorno, *Gesammelte Schriften*, VOL. 4., p. 95.

2. Adorno, *Minima Moralia*, p. 247.

3. Ibid.

4. Edmund Husserl, *Collected Works, Volume 7: Things and Space, Lectures of 1907* (Richard Rojcewicz trans.) (Dordrecht: Kluwer, 1997), pp. 19–20. On the 'phenomenological epoché', Husserl's Cartesian method of 'excluding' and 'parenthesizing', see Edmund Husserl, *Collected Works, Volume 2: Ideas Pertaining to a Pure Phenomenology and to a Phenomenological Philosophy* (F. Kersten trans.) (The Hague: Martinus Nijhoff, 1982), pp. 62ff. My disagreement with Husserl could be summarized like this.

First, that every possibility of insight or 'originary seizing upon [. . .] objectivities' (ibid., 66) which Husserl claims is a special achievement of the 'phenomenological attitude' in fact already belongs radically and inalienably to the so-called natural attitude; and second, that the 'phenomenological epoché' is not a reduction, as Husserl specifically conceived it, but an addition or gloss: the 'parenthesizing' of experience is essentially the superaddition of parentheses to experience. Neither of these mistakes, as I think of them, could seem tenable except for the prior misconception of doubt as something that may be 'precluded' by a calculistic 'reduction'.

5. Wordsworth, *Thirteen-Book Prelude*, VOL. 1, p. 229 (BK 8, lines 752–60); for the manuscripts transcription, cf. ibid., VOL. 2, p. 773 (BK 8, lines 754–5).

6. William Wordsworth, *Fourteen-Book Prelude* (W. J. B. Owen ed.) (Ithaca: Cornell University Press, 1985), p. 176.

7. A photograph of the manuscript page can be inspected in the *Thirteen-Book Prelude*, VOL. 2, p. 924. It is striking that the ink used for the revisions, that is, both the strikethroughs and the new words, is darker and considerably bolder than the ink that made the original lines, and that, unlike the ink of the original lines, the new ink bleeds on the paper so that the new words are somewhat more difficult to read than the old ones. This graphic aspect of the revision has the absorbing effect of making the now 'original' lines seem newly delicate and just faintly evanescent, so that it is difficult to avoid feeling that by revising the lines in a bolder hand Wordsworth

has overruled them, or at least that the later hand was possessed of an instrument of greater weight and authority, though of inferior accuracy. Both strikethroughs look from the photographs to be continuous and uninterrupted, so that Wordsworth must have known in advance of putting his pen to the paper that he would delete all the words which in the event he did delete.

8. 'I yearn towards some philosophic Song / Of Truth that cherishes our daily life' [Wordsworth, *Thirteen-Book Prelude*, VOL. 1, p. 112 (BK 1, lines 231–2). On philosophic song, cf. Simon Jarvis' *Wordsworth's Philosophic Song* (Cambridge: Cambridge University Press, 2007), whose discussion of these lines begins on the objective place, page 1.

9. Jordan, *De Quincey as Critic*, pp. 269ff.

10. Wordsworth, *Thirteen-Book Prelude*, VOL. 1, pp. 286–7 (BK 10, lines 709–27).

11. Ibid., VOL. 2, p. 883. For a photograph of the manuscript page, ibid., VOL. 1, p. 1050.

12. Ibid., VOL. 1, p. 295 (BK 11, lines 37–41).

13. Edward Young, *Night Thoughts* (Stephen Cornford ed.) (Cambridge: Cambridge University Press, 1989), p. 212.

14. Hugh Blair, *Sermons*, VOL. 5 (Edinburgh, 1777–1801), p. 167.

15. Samuel Johnson, *The Rambler, by Doctor Johnson, and Persian letters, by Lord Lyttleton* (London, 1800), p. 174.

16. William Gilpin, *An exposition of the New Testament; intended as an introduction to the study of the scriptures* (3rd edn), VOL. 2 (London, 1798), p. 409.

17. David Williams, *Lectures on the Universal Principles and Duties of Religion and Morality* (London, 1779), p. 15.

18. Wordsworth, *Thirteen-book Prelude*, VOL. 1, BK 1, line 311, and BK 5, line 474. I don't know what to make of this.

19. 'O Lady! we receive but what we give, / And in our life alone does Nature live' (Samuel Taylor Coleridge, 'Dejection: an Ode', lines 47–8).

Index